THE REMOVAL OF THE CHEROKEE NATION

Manifest Destiny or National Dishonor?

Problems in American Civilization

UNDER THE EDITORIAL DIRECTION OF

George Rogers Taylor

PURITANISM IN EARLY AMERICA

THE CAUSES OF THE AMERICAN REVOLUTION

BENJAMIN FRANKLIN AND THE AMERICAN CHARACTER

THE DECLARATION OF INDEPENDENCE AND THE CONSTITUTION

HAMILTON AND THE NATIONAL DEBT

THE TURNER THESIS CONCERNING THE ROLE OF THE FRONTIER IN AMERICAN HISTORY

THE GREAT TARIFF DEBATE, 1820–1830

THE REMOVAL OF THE CHEROKEE NATION — MANIFEST DESTINY OR NATIONAL DISHONOR?

JACKSON VERSUS BIDDLE — THE STRUGGLE OVER THE SECOND BANK OF THE UNITED STATES

THE TRANSCENDENTALIST REVOLT AGAINST MATERIALISM

THE COMPROMISE OF 1850

THE CAUSES OF THE AMERICAN CIVIL WAR

SLAVERY AS A CAUSE OF THE CIVIL WAR

LINCOLN AND THE COMING OF THE CIVIL WAR

THE AMERICANNESS OF WALT WHITMAN

RECONSTRUCTION IN THE SOUTH

MARK TWAIN'S *Huckleberry Finn*

DEMOCRACY AND THE GOSPEL OF WEALTH

JOHN D. ROCKEFELLER — ROBBER BARON OR INDUSTRIAL STATESMAN?

THE PULLMAN BOYCOTT OF 1894 — THE PROBLEM OF FEDERAL INTERVENTION

BOOKER T. WASHINGTON AND HIS CRITICS — THE PROBLEM OF NEGRO LEADERSHIP

WILLIAM JENNINGS BRYAN AND THE CAMPAIGN OF 1896

AMERICAN IMPERIALISM IN 1898

ROOSEVELT, WILSON, AND THE TRUSTS

PRAGMATISM AND AMERICAN CULTURE

WILSON AT VERSAILLES

THE NEW DEAL — REVOLUTION OR EVOLUTION?

FRANKLIN D. ROOSEVELT AND THE SUPREME COURT

PEARL HARBOR — ROOSEVELT AND THE COMING OF THE WAR

THE YALTA CONFERENCE

INDUSTRY-WIDE COLLECTIVE BARGAINING — PROMISE OE MENACE?

EDUCATION FOR DEMOCRACY — THE DEBATE OVER THE REPORT OF THE PRESIDENT'S COMMISSION ON HIGHER EDUCATION

EVOLUTION AND RELIGION — THE CONFLICT BETWEEN SCIENCE AND THEOLOGY IN MODERN AMERICA

IMMIGRATION — AN AMERICAN DILEMMA

LOYALTY IN A DEMOCRATIC STATE

DESEGREGATION AND THE SUPREME COURT

THE REMOVAL OF
THE CHEROKEE NATION:
Manifest Destiny or National Dishonor?

EDITED WITH AN INTRODUCTION BY

Louis Filler
ANTIOCH COLLEGE

AND

Allen Guttmann
AMHERST COLLEGE

Problems in American Civilization

READINGS SELECTED BY THE
DEPARTMENT OF AMERICAN STUDIES
AMHERST COLLEGE

ROBERT E. KRIEGER PUBLISHING COMPANY
HUNTINGTON, NEW YORK
1977

Original Edition 1962
Reprint 1977

Printed and Published by
ROBERT E. KRIEGER PUBLISHING CO., INC.
645 NEW YORK AVENUE
HUNTINGTON, NEW YORK 11743

Printed in the United States of America

Library of Congress Cataloging in Publication Data

Filler, Louis, 1911-   ed.
    The removal of the Cherokee Nation.

    Reprint of the edition published by Heath, Boston, in
series: Problems in American civilization.
    Bibliography: p.
    1. Cherokee Removal, 1838.   I. Guttmann, Allen,
joint ed.   II. Title.   III. Series: Problems in American
civilization.
[E99.C5F5   1977]   973.5'7   76-53820
ISBN 0-88275-482-3

PREFACE TO REPRINT EDITION

Since the original publication of this overview of the Cherokee problem as strategic to that of American Indians in general, there have been social developments which raise further questions about the place of Indians among other Americans. In effect, the old concept of Indians as "wards" of the American government has been rejected in modern times by a nation which posits not only equality for its several ethnic components, but "affirmative action" intended to overcome past circumstances derogatory of any one component, and limiting of its potential.

Nevertheless, questions persist regarding the preferences of any group, and their "potential" at least as related to those preferences. Original friends of the Cherokee sought to help them to attain the standards and preferences of non-Indians. Not a few Cherokee agreed with these goals and distinguished themselves in their pursuit; Sequoyah's is an immortal name among them. But many Cherokee found the social process debilitating. Moreover, they noted that it rarely brought them abreast of other Americans in social power and opportunity. In this respect Cherokee found themselves at one with other American Indian tribes which fought government troops across the Plains and into the far corners of the Northwest for their tribal customs and traditions, and were quelled by superior military forces.

A distinguished historian argued that sentimentalizing the Indians did not help their cause, and that Helen Hunt Jackson, for example (see pages 98-101), had ultimately distorted reality to no valid purpose.[1] Others have insisted that an evil condition requires darker hues of protest to dramatize the vital points of cruelty, greed, treachery, and ignorance, so that they all will stand out in ways appropriate to the conditions.

In either case, it would seem necessary for students to approach the task of understanding the American Indian question in terms of their interests and actual feelings, and those of their friends and foes. In a real sense, there are Indians; there is no "The Indian." Indian tribes inhabited and inhabit different regions. They possess different personalities, and often different goals. There are Indians, today, who wish to cling to the ways of their ancestors. It seems arrogant to attempt to persuade them in other directions. Other Indians, however, as groups and individuals ask for various "rights" based on concepts of natural or legal law. How are they to be best satisfied within the confines of a multi-ethnic nation all the components of which hunger for understanding and priority, and with numerous grievances often unknown to their neighbors or compatriots?

There is no simple answer to this question, other than that better knowledge gives promise of better solutions. This pamphlet has modest goals. It strives to contribute to an understanding of the dynamics which unfolded to one outstanding Indian tribe, and to keep the process undistorted.

LOUIS FILLER

Yellow Springs, Ohio
November, 1976

---

[1] Allan Nevins, "Helen Hunt Jackson, Sentimentalist vs. Realist," *American Scholar*, 10 (Summer, 1941), 269 ff.

INTRODUCTION

ON February 21, 1828, Elias Boudinot, a full-blooded Indian educated by Christian missionaries, published the first issue of *The Cherokee Phoenix*, a newspaper addressed to the Cherokee Nation. This first issue carried, in English and in the Cherokee alphabet invented by the celebrated Sequoyah, the text of a constitution adopted in July of the previous year. It seemed to the Rev. Samuel A. Worcester, the missionary who had suggested to Boudinot the name of the newspaper, that *The Cherokee Phoenix* was a symbol of the progress of the tribe. Under the protection of the United States, the Cherokees had adopted republican institutions and an agrarian way of life. Many of the Cherokees had been converted to Christianity. But most of the lands remaining to the Cherokee Nation lay within the boundaries of the State of Georgia, and the State of Georgia was determined to exercise its sovereignty. By January of 1832, Samuel Worcester was known to the world as one of the principals in *Worcester vs. The State of Georgia*, the Supreme Court case in which John Marshall attempted, unsuccessfully, to prevent the State from extending its laws throughout the Cherokee territory. During the fall and winter of 1838, the Cherokee Nation was gathered, under the guns of General Winfield Scott, and marched westward along paths that were to be known as "The Trail of Tears." The following years Elias Boudinot, who had counseled reluctant compliance with Georgia's demands, was assassinated by his own embittered people.

The clash between the Cherokee Nation and the State of Georgia was one which dramatized the problems inherent in the relations between Indian and white man. The conflict was, in addition, one which led quickly to a complex struggle between the State of Georgia and a Federal Government that was itself rent by divisions and disagreements. The questions raised by the conflict were perplexing ones. Could the Georgians, equalitarian and individualistic as they were, disregard the Supreme Court's interpretation of laws and treaties and still be considered "democratic"? Could Andrew Jackson, who refused to enforce Marshall's decision, lead the people in pursuit of their "Manifest Destiny" without sacrificing the very ideals which justified aggressive expansionism? On the other hand, could anyone expect the state of Georgia to tolerate an autonomous nation within her borders? Were the Cherokees, themselves the owners of Negro slaves, worth defending at the risk of a civil war? Finally, could Indians and white people ever, to use a term popular today, coexist?

John Marshall realized the gravity of these problems: "The legislative power of a state, the controlling power of the Constitution and laws of the United States, the rights, if they have any, the political existence of a once numerous and powerful people, the personal liberty of a citizen, are all involved in the subject now to be considered." Before attempting to decide *Worcester vs. The State of Georgia*, Marshall reviewed the events which had led to the case before him. This is, roughly, the method adopted in this collection of documents. Except for Ulrich Bonnell Phillips' "Expulsion of the Cherokees," which provides a concise historical framework, the readings are grouped so that the conflict develops chronologically along the lines drawn in the 1820's and 1830's by the participants in the conflict.

Taking office in 1829, Andrew Jackson, himself a symbol of the American frontier and its new political importance, changed the emphases of the Indian policies of John Quincy Adams, his predecessor in office. Jackson's first Annual Message, from which "The Condition and Ulterior Destiny of the Indians" is taken, marked a new era. That Georgia realized this is clear from the next selection, the Georgia Law of December 19, 1829. Meanwhile, Wilson Lumpkin, Georgia's representative on the House of Representatives' Committee on Indian Affairs, went to work on legislation authorizing further Indian removal. The bill reported to the House (February 24, 1830) touched off an acrimonious debate in both houses of Congress. Senator Theodore Frelinghuysen—like Adams, of an old American family—made the most noted speech against removal, but Edward Everett and other New Englanders joined him in opposing Lumpkin's bill. In the House, Lumpkin himself pled Georgia's case. Born in Virginia, reared on the Georgia frontier, leader of the small-farmer or "Clarke" faction in state politics, Lumpkin seems to provide clear evidence respecting the attitudes toward Indians of some frontiersmen. The following selection, however, is from a speech by the man who

has rivaled Dan'l Boone for the title of American Frontiersman—the Honorable David Crockett of Tennessee. No one in America was further removed in character and in habits from the Everetts and Adamses and Frelinghuysens, and Crockett's remarks add a certain complexity to an already complex situation. Lumpkin's bill passed.

The Cherokee Indians speak for themselves; their "Memorial" to Congress indicates that they were well able to do so. In their appeals, they were supported by a number of missionaries, some of whom had spent a decade or more among the tribe. Through these missionaries and through *The Cherokee Phoenix,* the Indians were able to reach a wide audience.

The appeals of the Cherokees and of the missionaries were in vain. Jackson's second Annual Message was less conciliatory than his first had been. The Indians turned to the courts. John Marshall's decision in *The Cherokee Nation vs. Georgia* is printed as the next selection. The decision was a disappointment to the Indians, but it did not indicate that Marshall's Court approved of all that the Georgians had done, nor, as Justice Thompson's dissenting opinion makes clear, did all of "Marshall's" Court agree with the Chief Justice in his decision. The State of Georgia pressed forward its claims and demanded that all whites residing in Indian territory be licensed by the State. The Rev. Samuel Worcester, who had signed the "Memorial" and established himself as a leader of the missionaries, refused to secure such a license. He was arrested and, eventually, found guilty by Georgia courts. At this point, Marshall interposed and overruled the Georgia law and declared it void. Andrew Jackson is reported to have said,

"John Marshall has made his decision; now let him enforce it." Jackson's behavior attests to the symbolic if not to the actual truth of the anecdote. Ex-Governor George M. Troup, then serving as United States Senator, defied the Court in an open letter to the people of Georgia; the letter is printed after Marshall's decision in the Worcester case. Troup's stand was strongly seconded by Wilson Lumpkin, then governor of Georgia, in his message to the Georgia legislature. The State was triumphant. The Treaty of New Echota (1835) was imposed upon the Cherokees with the reluctant assent of a minority of the tribe. In 1838, the Indians were removed by General Winfield Scott.

The next selection is from a sharp-tongued foreign observer, Mrs. Frances M. Trollope. Her comments are representative of the general European response to American policy. Alexis de Tocqueville, the author of one of the most perceptive books ever written about the United States, delved beneath the immediate details and uncovered some of the implications which lay at the heart of the matter. His comments, taken from the last chapter of *Democracy in America,* follow Mrs. Trollope's.

Americans were not silent. Ralph Waldo Emerson, one of the most unpolitical of our philosophers, was moved, in 1838, to write an "Open Letter" to President Martin Van Buren. In 1881, Helen Hunt Jackson, formerly of Massachusetts, protested our state and federal Indian policies in *A Century of Dishonor,* the classic indictment. Such appeals were in vain. Americans pursued their "Manifest Destiny," and the Indian tribes were forced either to give up their lands by treaty or to lose them after armed resistance led to military defeat.

The last two selections are from twentieth-century historians. Frederick Jackson Turner's defense of Andrew Jackson is a reluctant one based on Turner's own belief in frontier democracy. E. Merton Coulter's defense is a more belligerent justification of Georgia's pursuit of her destiny.

Although this selection of readings ends with the statements of those who remain in possession of the field, the controversy over the "Indian Question" continues. The removal policy was, eventually, abandoned. The reservation policy, in its turn, was combined with a policy of assimilation. Should it succeed, the Indian will have ceased to be a problem.

Nevertheless, historians continue to dispute the relative merits of Cherokees and Georgians, and Edmund Wilson's recent *Apologies to the Iroquois* reminds us that some white people still feel a guilt or a doubt which practical arguments seem not to lessen. Was injustice done to the Cherokees? On what grounds can the decisions made by Chief Justice Marshall or by President Jackson or by Governor Lumpkin be justified? Moreover, the State of Georgia still differs with the Supreme Court over difficulties caused by ethnic difference and minority status, and warfare in Asia and Africa reminds us of the heritage of European imperialism. To what degree does a study of Indian removal aid us in resolving the problems of segregation in the South (and in the North)? What obligations have nations today toward aboriginal populations in colonial or semicolonial areas? Have we, the democratic societies of the "Atlantic Community," made adequate progress in our treatment of racial and other minority groups, or must these groups turn elsewhere for an answer to *their* appeals and resolutions and memorials?

CONTENTS

Preparing to annex the Indian lands, Georgia extends her laws throughout the Cherokee territory:

> And be it . . . enacted, That after the first day of June next, all laws, ordinances, orders and regulations of any kind whatever, made, passed, or enacted by the Cherokee Indians . . . are hereby declared to be null and void and of no effect, as if the same had never existed . . . .

The Cherokees protest:

> We wish to remain on the land of our fathers. We have a perfect and original right to remain without interruption or molestation. The treaties with us, and laws of the United States made in pursuance of treaties, guaranty our residence and our privileges, and secure us against intruders.

And the Supreme Court upholds the rights of the Cherokees:

> The Cherokee nation . . . is a distinct community, occupying its own territories, with boundaries accurately described, in which the laws of Georgia can have no force, and which the citizens of Georgia have no right to enter . . . .
>
> —JOHN MARSHALL

But, with President Jackson's tacit approval, the Governor of Georgia defies the Supreme Court:

> The ingenuity of man might be challenged to show a single sentence of the Constitution of the United States giving power, either direct or implied, to the general government . . . to nullify the laws of a State . . . or coerce obedience, by force, to the mandates of the judiciary of the Union.
>
> —WILSON LUMPKIN

The Indians are removed from Georgia, and a New Englander writes in condemnation:

> In the whole history of our Government's dealings with the Indian tribes, there is no record so black as the record of its perfidy to [the Cherokee] nation.
>
> —HELEN HUNT JACKSON

But a Southern historian justifies the policy of Indian removal:

> This threat of being deprived of a great part of her domain by an alien and semi-barbarous people appeared intolerable and unthinkable to Georgia. . . . [She] forbade the Indians to play with their make-believe government. . . . With the Indians finally out of the way, Georgia was for the first time in her existence master of her own territorial destiny.
>
> —E. MERTON COULTER

Ulrich Bonnell Phillips:

THE EXPULSION OF THE CHEROKEES

*Although the reputation of Ulrich Bonnell Phillips is based primarily upon his two studies of slavery—*American Negro Slavery (1918) *and* Life and Labor in the Old South (1929)—*he first received notice as a historian of his native Georgia. His monograph,* Georgia and State Rights, *was awarded the Justin Winsor Prize of the American Historical Association. The selection which follows is from this book. It provides an accurate and useful account of the facts of Cherokee expulsion.*

AT the beginning of the American Revolution the hunting grounds of the Cherokees were conceded to extend from the eastern slopes of the Blue Ridge to the neighborhood of the Mississippi River and from the Ohio River almost as far south as central Georgia. Most of their villages, however, were located in eastern Tennessee and northern Georgia. The settlement of the country by the whites, and the acquisitions of the Indian territory by them, was naturally along the lines of least resistance. That is to say, the Cherokees first ceded away their remote hunting grounds and held most tenaciously to the section in which their towns were situated.

At an early stage in the Revolution a body of militia from the Southern States made a successful attack upon the eastern villages of the Cherokees, who were in alliance with the British. The tribe was at once ready for peace, and signed a treaty with commissioners from Georgia and South Carolina at Dewits Corner, on May 20, 1777, acknowledging defeat at the hands of the Americans, establishing peace, and yielding their title to a section of their lands, lying chiefly in South Carolina.

The Cherokee families which had lived upon the lands conquered now moved westward, extending the settlements of the tribe farther along the course of the Tennessee River. At the same time five new villages were built by the most warlike part of the nation on Chickamauga Creek and in the neighboring district southeast of Lookout Mountain. Before the end of the Revolution the Cherokees were again at war with the Americans, and Gen. Elijah Clarke led an expedition against this settlement on the Chickamauga. The sudden raid caused such terror in the Indian villages that the inhabitants eagerly promised great cessions of land in order to be rid of the invaders. Clarke

U. B. Phillips, "The Expulsion of the Cherokees," from *Georgia & State Rights* (Washington: U.S. Gov. Printing Office, 1902), pp. 66–86. For complete footnotes in this and other selections, see original publications.

made what he called a treaty at Long Swamp, but the agreement was necessarily informal and extra-legal. The fact that it was not followed up by the proper authorities caused Clarke to think that the people had not benefited sufficiently by his exertions. The injury to his feelings in this connection was probably responsible in part for his attempted settlement on Indian lands in 1794.

At the close of the Revolution, the Cherokees ceded to Georgia their claim to a district about the sources of the Oconee, which they held as hunting ground in joint possession with the Creeks. In the territory which the Cherokees retained, the districts near the Georgia settlements were less attractive than the Creek lands to the south. The upland region in the State was being rapidly settled, however, and new lands were in demand. The State made occasional attempts between 1785 and 1800 to obtain further cessions. Frequent conventions were held by commissioners of the United States and the Cherokee chieftains, at some of which representatives of Georgia were present. But the tribe held fast to its Georgia lands. By the treaty of Hopewell in 1785 the Cherokee Nation placed itself under the protection of the United States and agreed to specified boundaries for its territory, but it made no cession which concerned Georgia. The agreement of Hopewell was confirmed at a convention on the Holston River in 1791, and again at Philadelphia in 1793, but the boundaries on the southeast remained practically unchanged.[1]

The treaty of Philadelphia was rendered necessary by hostilities arising with the tribe in 1793; the Chickamauga towns, as usual, provoked the unpleas-

antness on the Indian side, while the settlers on the frontier of North Carolina and Tennessee were quite as much to blame on the side of the whites. Considerable excitement prevailed for several months, and raids were made by each party; but the fact that the Creek country intervened between Georgia and the chief settlements of the Cherokees directed the warlike energies of the tribe to the north and northeast.

After 1795 no considerable portion of the Cherokee Nation was at any time seriously inclined to war. Those of its members who preferred the life of hunters moved away to the Far West, while the bulk of the tribe remaining settled down to the pursuit of agriculture. The chief complaint which Georgia could make of them in later years was that they kept possession of the soil, while white men wanted to secure it for themselves.

The invention of the cotton gin in 1793 had the effect after a few years of increasing the preference of the Georgians for the warm and fertile Creek lands, over the Cherokee territory which was ill adapted to cotton with the then prevailing system of agriculture. For this reason it was not until all of the Creek lands had been secured for settlement that the State authorities began to make strenuous efforts for the expulsion of the Cherokees. In the intervening years certain moderate steps were taken, which must now engage our attention.

As early as 1803 Thomas Jefferson suggested the advisability of removing all of the southern Indians west of the Mississippi, and in 1809 a delegation of Cherokees, at the instance of the United States Indian agent, Return J. Meigs, made a visit to the Western lands. At that time a considerable part of the Cherokee Nation favored removal, but the matter was postponed. General An-

[1] *American State Papers: Indian Affairs*, I, 83, 124, and 543.

drew Jackson reported, in 1816, that the whole nation would soon offer to move West. When negotiations were made for a treaty in the next year it was found that there was a division of opinion. The Lower Cherokees, who lived chiefly in Georgia, were disposed to emigrate, while the Upper or Tennessee division of the nation preferred to remain and to change from their wild life to the pursuit of agriculture. By the treaty signed at the Cherokee Agency, July 8, 1817, a tract of land was ceded in Georgia, and arrangement was made that such Indian families as so desired might take up new homes in the Far West.[2]

Within the next two years about one-third of the Cherokees moved into the Louisiana Territory; but it happened quite unexpectedly that each section of the nation had altered its disposition, so that a large part of the Upper Cherokees moved away from Tennessee, while most of the Lower Cherokees remained in Georgia. Thus, when a treaty came to be made in 1819, it was found that a large area had been vacated to the north and east, but only a small district could be obtained in Georgia. It further appeared that, owing to the influence of a powerful chief named Hicks, the westward movement had almost completely stopped.[3]

The treaties of 1817 and 1819 provided that the head of any Cherokee family living in the district ceded to the United States might at his option remain in possession of his home, together with 640 acres of land, which should descend to his heirs in fee simple. The Georgia legislature, of course, protested against this provision as violative of the rights of the State, while Congressional committees declared that in so far as the treaty provided for Indians to become citizens, it infringed upon the powers of Congress.[4] The agreement was accordingly modified and the Cherokee family holdings were gradually purchased during the next few years.

Georgia was at this period beginning to grow insistent upon obtaining possession of the Cherokee lands as well as those of the Creeks. In March of 1820, President Monroe requested appropriations from Congress to extinguish by treaty the Indian title to all lands in Georgia. When the Cherokees were officially approached upon the subject in 1823, the council of chiefs replied to the commissioners, Messrs. Campbell and Merriwether: "It is the fixed and unalterable determination of this nation never again to cede one foot more of our land." That part of the tribe which had emigrated had suffered severely from sickness, wars, and other calamities, and the remainder refused to follow them. To emphasize their decision a delegation proceeded to Washington, where they declared to the President that, "the Cherokees are not foreigners, but the original inhabitants of America, and that they now stand on the soil of their own territory, and they can not recognize the sovereignty of any State within the limits of their territory."[5]

It may easily be surmised that the chiefs who delivered this declaration were not full-blooded, wild Indians. As a matter of fact, the average member of the tribe, while not savage, was heavy and stupid; but the nation was

[2] *Indian Affairs*, II, 125 and 129.
[3] *Indian Affairs*, II, 187, 188, 259, and 462. O. H. Prince, *Laws of Georgia to 1820*, p. 321.
[4] U.S. House Journal, 16th Cong., 1st sess., p. 336. Prince, *Laws of Georgia to 1820*, p. 531.
[5] U.S. House Journal, 16th Cong., 1st sess., p. 315 (Mar. 17, 1820). *Indian Affairs*, II, 468 and 474.

under the complete control of its chiefs, who were usually half-breeds, or white men married into the nation. Many of these chiefs were intelligent and wealthy, but their followers continued to live from hand to mouth, with little ambition to better themselves. Each family cultivated a small field, and perhaps received a pittance from the annual subsidy of the United States; but, as a rule, the payments for cessions of land never percolated deeper than the stratum of the lesser chiefs. The attitude of the United States had undergone a great change. Formerly the tribes near the frontiers had been held as terrible enemies, but they had now become objects of commiseration. The policy of the Government had once been to weaken these tribes, but that had given place to the effort to civilize them.[6]

It is remarkable that the United States Government was still inclined to regard the Indian tribes in the light of sovereign nations. The Cherokee delegation was received at Washington in 1824 with diplomatic courtesy, and its representations attended to as those of a foreign power. The Congressional Representatives of Georgia viewed the matter from the standpoint of their State. They accordingly remonstrated with the President, March 10, 1824, against the practice of showing diplomatic courtesy to the Cherokees. They said that too much time had been wasted, while the Indians were further than ever from removal. If a peaceable purchase of the Cherokee land could not be made, they demanded that the nation be peremptorily ordered to remove and suitably indemnified for their pains.

Mr. Monroe replied in a message to Congress on March 30 that the United States had done its best in the past to carry out the agreement of 1802, and that the Government was under no obligation to use other means than peaceable and reasonable ones. Governor Troup entered his protest against the message on April 24, urging that Georgia had the sole right to the lands, and denying that the Indians were privileged to refuse when a cession was demanded. The Cherokees, for their part, held to their contention for national rights, appealing to the clause in the Declaration of Independence "that all men are created equal," and reiterating their determination to give up not an inch of their land.[7] As far as concerned results, the Cherokees had the best of the argument. The effort to drive them west was given up for a time.

The delegation returned home to lead their tribesmen still further in the ways of civilization. A Cherokee alphabet was devised by Sequoyah in 1825, a printing press was set up at the capital, New Echota, in the following year, and soon afterward steps were taken to formulate a written constitution for the nation. Meanwhile the Cherokee population was increasing with considerable rapidity. In 1818 an estimate had been made which placed the number east of the Mississippi at 10,000, and it was thought that 5,000 were living on the Western lands. A census was taken in 1825 of the Cherokee Nation in the East. Of native citizens there were numbered 13,563; of white men and women married in the nations, 147 and 73, respectively; of negro slaves, 1,277.

The Cherokee national constitution was adopted in a convention of repre-

[6] Message of Governor Gilmer, Dec. 6, 1830, *Niles's Register*, XXXIX, 339. Cf. Letter of Supt. of Indian Affairs to Sec. of War, Mar. 1, 1826, *Indian Affairs*, II, 658.

[7] *Niles's Register*, XXVI, 100, 103. *Indian Affairs*, III, 476, 502, 736.

sentatives on July 26, 1827. It asserted that the Cherokee Indians constituted one of the sovereign and independent nations of the earth, having complete jurisdiction over its territory, to the exclusion of the authority of any other State, and it provided for a representative system of government, modeled upon that of the United States.[8]

Of course Georgia could not countenance such a procedure. Governor Troup had just worsted President Adams in the controversy over the Creek lands, and the State was prepared at least to hold its own against the Cherokees. The legislature, on December 27, adopted resolutions of no doubtful tenor. After praising Governor Troup for his able and patriotic conduct regarding the Creek lands, the preamble showed that since the agreement of 1802 the Indians had been removed entirely from Ohio, Kentucky, North and South Carolina, Tennessee, and Missouri, from nearly all of Arkansas and Alabama, and that large cessions had been obtained in Mississippi, Illinois, Michigan, and Florida. The resolutions followed: "That the policy which has been pursued by the United States toward the Cherokee Indians has not been in good faith toward Georgia. . . . That all the lands, appropriated and unappropriated, which lie within the conventional limits of Georgia belong to her absolutely; that the title is in her; that the Indians are tenants at her will, . . . and that Georgia has the right to extend her authority and her laws over her whole territory and to coerce obedience to them from all descriptions of people, be they white, red, or black, who may reside within her limits." The document closed with the statement that violence would not be used to secure Georgia's rights until other means should have failed.[9]

When a year had passed with no developments in furtherance of the policy of the State, Governor Forsyth advised the passage of an act to extend the laws of Georgia over the Cherokee territory, but suggested that such law should not take effect until the President should have had time again to urge the Indians to emigrate. The legislature accordingly, by an act of December 20, 1828, carried out its threat of the previous year, enacting that all white persons in the Cherokee territory should be subject to the laws of Georgia, providing that after June 1, 1830, all Indians resident therein should be subject to such laws as might be prescribed for them by the State, and declaring that after that date all laws made by the Cherokee Nation should be null and void.[10]

Before any further legislative steps were taken, a new and unexpected development arose which tended to hasten some early solution of the complex problem. In July, 1829, deposits of gold were found in the northeastern corner of the State, and the news rapidly spread that the fields were as rich as those being worked in North Carolina. As soon as the news was known to be authentic there came a rush of adventurers into the gold lands. In the summer of 1830 there were probably 3,000 men from various States digging gold in Cherokee Georgia. The intrusion of these miners into the Cherokee territory was unlawful under the enactments of three several governments, each claiming juris-

[8] *Indian Affairs*, II, 651, 652. Royce, *The Cherokee Nation*, p. 241.

[9] Acts of Georgia General Assembly, 1827, p. 249. For text of Cherokee constitution see U.S. Executive Document No. 91, 23rd Cong., 2d sess., vol. 3. *Cherokee Phoenix*, Feb. 28, 1828.
[10] *Athenian*, Nov. 18, 1828. Dawson, *Compilation of Georgia Laws*, p. 198. Prince, *Digest of the Laws of Georgia to 1837*, p. 278.

diction over the region. The United States laws prohibited anyone from settling or trading on Indian territory without a special license from the proper United States official; the State of Georgia had extended its laws over the Cherokee lands, applying them, after June 1, 1830, to Indians as well as white men; the Cherokee Nation had passed a law that no one should settle or trade on their lands without a permit from their officials.[11]

A conflict of authorities was imminent, and yet at that time no one of the three governments, nor, indeed, all of them combined, had sufficient police service in the section to check the great disorder which prevailed. The government of Georgia was the first of the three to make an efficient attempt to meet the emergency. Governor Gilmer wrote to the President October 29, 1830, stating that the Cherokee lands had been put under the laws of Georgia, and asking that the United States troops be withdrawn.

General Jackson, whose view of the Indian controversy was radically opposed to that of Mr. Adams, did not hesitate to reverse the policy of the Government. He had already expressed his belief that Georgia had a rightful jurisdiction over her Indian lands, and he lost no time in complying with Mr. Gilmer's request to withdraw his troops. The general assembly of Georgia was called in special session in October for the purpose of making additional laws for the regulation of the gold region. By an act of December 22, 1830, a guard of 60 men was established to prevent intrusion and disorder at the gold mines. By the same act it was made unlawful

for any Cherokee council or legislative body to meet, except for the purpose of ceding land, while the same penalty of four years' imprisonment was fixed to punish any Cherokee officials who should presume to hold a court. Not content with this, the legislature enacted by the same law that all white persons resident in the Cherokee territory on March 1, 1831, or after, without a license from the governor of Georgia or his agent, should be guilty of a high misdemeanor, with the penalty provided of not less than four years' confinement in the penitentiary. The governor was empowered to grant licenses to those who should take an oath to support and defend the constitution and laws of Georgia, and uprightly to demean themselves as citizens of the State.[12]

The attitude of the judge of the Georgia superior court, who had most of the Cherokee territory in his circuit, had already been shown in a letter which he, Judge A. S. Clayton, wrote Governor Gilmer June 22, 1830, suggesting a request to the President for the withdrawal of the United States troops. Nine citizens of Hall County had just been brought before him by the Federal troops for trespassing on the Cherokee territory. He wrote: "When I saw the honest citizens of your State paraded through the streets of our town, in the center of a front and rear guard of regular troops, belonging, if not to a foreign, at least to another government, . . . for no other crime than that of going upon soil of their own State, . . . I confess to you I never so distinctly felt, as strong as my feelings have been on that subject, the deep

---

[11] Athenian, August 4, 1829. Georgia Journal, September 4, 1830. G. White, Historical Collections of Georgia, p. 136.

[12] Athenian, October 19 and 26, 1830. Niles's Register, XXXIX, 263. Acts of Georgia Gen. Assem., 1830, p. 114. Prince, Digest of Georgia Laws to 1837, p. 279. Georgia Journal, January 1, 1831.

humiliation of our condition in relation to the exercise of power on the part of the General Government within the jurisdiction of Georgia."[13]

Three months later Judge Clayton, in a charge to the grand jury of Clarke County, expressed his belief in the constitutionality of the recent extension of Georgia's laws, and his intention to enforce it. He said that he would disregard any interference of the United States Supreme Court in cases which might arise before him from the act of Georgia. "I only require the aid of public opinion and the arm of the executive authority," he concluded, "and no court on earth besides our own shall ever be troubled with this question."[14]

It was with good reason that the State officials were determined if possible to keep the Cherokee questions out of the Federal courts. The policy of Chief Justice John Marshall was known to be that of consolidating the American nation by a broad interpretation of the Federal Constitution, and a consequent restriction of the sphere of the State governments.

The Cherokee chiefs had learned to their sorrow that President Jackson readily conceded all that Mr. Adams had struggled to deny to Georgia. The hostile legislation of Georgia had paralyzed the working of the Cherokee constitution. The President admitted the right of the State to survey the Indian lands, to extend its laws over them, and to annul the laws of the Cherokees. He refused to recognize the Cherokee constitution and denied that the nation had any rights as opposed to Georgia. With

such cold comfort from the Executive, the chiefs determined to resort to the judicial branch of the Federal Government in a final effort to save their homes from the rapacity of Georgia. . . .

The opinion of the court [in The Cherokee Nation *v.* Georgia], as rendered by Chief Justice Marshall, granted that the counsel for the plaintiffs had established that the Cherokee Nation was a State and had been treated as a State since the settlement of the colonies; but the majority of the court decided that an Indian tribe or nation in the United States was not a foreign state in the sense of the Constitution and could not maintain an action in the courts of the United States. The decision concluded accordingly, "If it be true that the Cherokee Nation have rights, this is not the tribunal in which those rights are to be asserted. If it be true that wrongs have been inflicted and that still greater are to be apprehended, this is not the tribunal which can redress the past or prevent the future. The motion for an injunction is denied."

In a separate opinion Mr. Justice Johnson held that the name "State" should not be given to a people so low in grade of organized society as were the Indian tribes. He contended . . . that the United States allotted certain lands to the Cherokees, intending to give them no more rights over the territory than those needed by hunters, concluding that every advance of the Indians in civilization must tend to impair the right of preemption, which was of course a right of the State of Georgia.

Mr. Justice Thompson gave a dissenting opinion, in which Mr. Justice Story concurred, that the Cherokee Nation was competent to sue in the court and

---

[13] The original of this letter is among the archives in the State Capitol, Atlanta, Ga. (MSS).
[14] *Niles's Register,* XXXVIII, 101.

the desired injunction ought to be awarded.

It was clear that nowhere in the opinion of the court was it stated that the extension of the laws of Georgia over the Cherokee territory was valid and constitutional. This one case had been thrown out of court because no standing in court could be conceded to the plaintiffs. The decision was against the Cherokee Nation for the time being; but it did not necessarily follow that a subsequent decision would bear out the claims of the State of Georgia.

Messrs. Wirt and Sergeant had brought their action against the State of Georgia in the name of the Cherokee Nation only because no promising opportunity for making a personal case had arisen. One of the complaints in the bill for injunction was that the cases where the Georgia laws operated in the Cherokee territory were allowed to drag in the Georgia courts so as to prevent any one of the Cherokee defendants from carrying his case to the United States Supreme Court by writ of error. An attempt had been made to utilize the Tassel case, but the prompt execution of the criminal put an early end to the project. The first case which arose of a character suitable for the purpose of the attorneys was upon the conviction of Samuel A. Worcester for illegal residence in the Cherokee territory. The history of the case was as follows:

The act of the Georgia legislature approved December 22, 1830, which we have noticed, made it unlawful for white persons to reside in the Cherokee territory in Georgia without having taken an oath of allegiance to the State and without a license from the State authorities. This law was directed primarily against the intruding gold miners; but the message of the governor had stated the expediency of considering all white persons as intruders, without regard to the length of their residence or the permission of the Indians. The law was accordingly made one of sweeping application.

There were at the time resident among the Cherokees twelve or more Christian missionaries and assistants, some of them maintained by the American Board of Commissioners for Foreign Missions. These men were already suspected of interfering in political matters and would probably have been made to feel the weight of the law without inviting attention to themselves, but they did not passively await its action. They held a meeting at New Echota December 29, 1830, in which they passed resolutions protesting the extension of the laws of Georgia over the Indians and asserting that they considered the removal of the Cherokees an event most earnestly to be deprecated.[15]

After sufficient time had elapsed for the intruders to have taken their departure, if so disposed, the Georgia guard for the Cherokee territory arrested such white men as were found unlawfully residing therein. Among the number arrested were two missionaries, Messrs. Worcester and Thompson. On writ of habeas corpus they were taken before the superior court of Gwinnett County, where their writ was passed upon by Judge Clayton. Their counsel pleaded for their release upon the ground of the unconstitutionality of the law of Georgia. The judge granted their release, but did so upon the ground that they were agents of the United States, since they were expend-

[15] *Athenian,* January 25, 1831. White, *Historical Collections of Georgia,* p. 139.

ing the United States fund for civilizing the Indians. Governor Gilmer then sent inquiries to Washington to learn whether the missionaries were recognized agents of the Government. The reply was received that as missionaries they were not governmental agents, but that Mr. Worcester was United States Postmaster at New Echota. President Jackson, upon request from Georgia, removed Mr. Worcester from that office in order to render him amenable to the laws of the State. The *Cherokee Phoenix*, the newspaper and organ of the nation, expressed outraged feelings on the part of the Indians at the combination of the State and Federal executives against them.

The governor wrote Mr. Worcester, May 16, advising his removal from the State to avoid arrest. May 28, Col. J. W. A. Sandford, commander of the Georgia Guard, wrote each of the missionaries that at the end of ten days he would arrest them if found upon Cherokee territory in Georgia. Notwithstanding their address to the governor in justification of their conduct, they were arrested by the guard, the Rev. Samuel A. Worcester, the Rev. Elizur Butler, and the Rev. James Trott, missionaries, and eight other white men, for illegal residence in the territory. Their trial came on in the September term of the Gwinnett County superior court. They were found guilty, and on September 15 were each sentenced to four years' confinement at hard labor in the State penitentiary. But a pardon and freedom were offered to each by the governor on condition of taking the oath of allegiance or promising to leave the Cherokee territory. Nine of the prisoners availed themselves of the executive clemency, but Worcester and Butler chose rather to go to the penitentiary,

intending to test their case before the Supreme Court.[16]

On the occasion of their second arrest the missionaries had been taken into custody by a section of the Georgia Guard, commanded by a subordinate officer, Colonel Nelson. During the journey from the scene of the arrest to the place of temporary confinement the treatment of the prisoners was needlessly rough, extending in the cases of Messrs. Worcester and McLeod to positive harshness and violence. These two clergymen complained to the head of their missionary board of having been put in shackles, and of other indignities. The State government condemned the severity of the guard, and ordered an inquiry made into Nelson's conduct. That officer explained that his course of action had been rendered necessary by the unruly character of his prisoners. The controversy was practically closed by the retort of the Rev. Mr. McLeod that Colonel Nelson's statements were false and his conduct villainous.[17]

The cases of Worcester and Butler, who refused the governor's conditions for pardon, were appealed to the United States Supreme Court, from which a writ of error was issued on October 27, 1831.

Wilson Lumpkin, who had become governor of Georgia, submitted to the legislature on November 25, 1831, copies of the citations of the United States Supreme Court to the State of Georgia to appear and show cause why the judgments which had been made against Worcester and Butler should not be set aside. With the documents went a mes-

16 White, *Historical Collections of Georgia*, p. 140. *Niles's Register*, XL, 296. Georgia *Journal*, Sept. 29, 1831.

17 Georgia *Journal*, Oct. 6, 1831, and Dec. 5, 1831.

sage: "In exercising the duties of that department of the government which devolves upon me, I will disregard all unconstitutional requisitions, of whatever character or origin they may be, and, to the best of my abilities, will protect and defend the rights of the State, and use the means afforded me to maintain its laws and constitution."

The legislature on December 26 adopted resolutions upholding the constitutionality and the soundness of policy in the recent enactments of the State, declaring that it had become a question of abandoning the attempt to remove the Indians or of excluding from residence among the nation of white persons whose efforts were known to be in opposition to the policy of the State. Regarding the citation received, the legislature resolved, "That the State of Georgia will not compromit her dignity as a sovereign State, or so far yield her rights as a member of the Confederacy as to appear in, answer to, or in any way become a party to any proceedings before the Supreme Court having for their object a revisal or interference with the decisions of the State courts in criminal matters."[18]

The hearing on the writ of error in Worcester's case came up before the Supreme Court during the course of the year 1832. . . . The conclusion was reached that "the Cherokee Nation, then, is a distinct community, occupying its own territory, with boundaries accurately described, in which the laws of Georgia can have no force. . . . The act of the State of Georgia, under which the plaintiff was prosecuted, is consequently void, and the judgment a nullity. It is the opinion of the court that the judgment of the Georgia county

superior court ought to be reversed and annulled." The case of Butler v. Georgia, similar in all respects to that of Worcester, was in effect decided in the same manner by the opinion rendered in Worcester's case.

The judgment for which the Cherokees had so long been hoping was thus finally rendered; but they rejoiced too soon if they thought that by virtue of it their troubles were at an end. Governor Lumpkin declared to the legislature, November 6, 1832, that the decision of the court was an attempt to "prostrate the sovereignty of this State in the exercise of its constitutional criminal jurisdiction," an attempt at usurpation which the State executive would meet with the spirit of determined resistance. He congratulated himself that the people of Georgia were unanimous in "sustaining the sovereignty of their State."[19]

The unchanged attitude of Georgia boded ill for the hopes of the Cherokees. But the position of the Federal Executive rendered the situation desperate in the last degree for those Indians who were still determined not to give up their homes. President Jackson simply refused to enforce the judgment of the Supreme Court. He intimated that now that John Marshall had rendered his decision, he might enforce it. Of course the chief justice had no authority beyond stating what he thought right in the case. Worcester and Butler remained at hard labor in the Georgia penitentiary, and the Cherokee chiefs began at length to realize that no recourse was left them against the tyranny of the State.

As far as the two missionaries were concerned, they felt that their martyrdom had been sufficiently long, and

18 *Niles's Register*, XLI, 313. Acts of Georgia General Assembly, 1831, pp. 259, 268.

19 *Niles's Register*, XLIII, 206.

adopted the course of conciliating the State in order to secure their liberation. They informed the attorney-general of Georgia on January 8, 1833, that they had instructed their counsel to prosecute their case no further in the Supreme Court. Appreciating the change in their attitude, Governor Lumpkin pardoned both of them January 10 on the same conditions that he had offered them some months before, and ordered their release from prison.[20]

Most of the people of Georgia approved of the pardoning of Worcester and Butler under the circumstances, but that action of the governor found many critics among the ultramontanists. A meeting of citizens of Taliaferro County, which lay in the center of the hothead section, resolved, on April 23, 1833, with only one dissenting vote, "That the executive of Georgia, in the case of the missionaries, did, by his conduct, sacrifice the dignity of the State and prove himself incapable of sustaining her honor. . . . Resolved, further, that there is no one so well qualified to repair the tarnished honor of the State as our patriotic fellow-citizen, George M. Troup."

The attacks upon Mr. Lumpkin grew so strong that in view of his prospective candidacy for a second term as governor his friends saw fit to publish the various documents and considerations which had led to the release of the two missionaries.[21]

In the course of the year 1834 a final tilt occurred between the State of Georgia and the Cherokee Nation, supported by the Supreme Court. . . . A citation of the Supreme Court, dated October 28, 1834, summoned the State of Georgia to appear and show cause why the error shown in the writ of error in the case of James Graves, tried and convicted of murder, should not be corrected. On November 7 Mr. Lumpkin sent a copy of the citation to the legislature, stating that it constituted a third attempt to control the State in the exercise of its ordinary criminal jurisdiction. "Such attempts, if persevered in," he said, "will eventuate in the dismemberment and overthrow of our great confederacy. . . . I shall . . . to the utmost of my power, protect and defend the rights of the State." The legislature adopted resolutions which it considered appropriate to the occasion, referring to the "residuary mass of sovereignty which is inherent in each State . . . in the confederacy."[22] Graves was executed in due time, according to the sentence of the Georgia court.

The case of Graves was superfluous so far as it concerned the status of the Cherokee Nation. The fiasco of the decision in Worcester's case established the permanent triumph of Georgia's policy, and rendered it only a question of a very few years when the Indians would be driven from their territory within the limits of the State.

As far as regards the Federal Executive, the government of Georgia stood upon the vantage ground, after 1827, which it had won by its victory over Mr. Adams. General Jackson approved of the contention of the State, and from the time of his inauguration used his influence for the removal of the Indians. In a message of December 8, 1829, he stated, in reply to the Cherokee protest against the extension of Georgia laws over them, that the attempt by the Indians to establish an independent

[20] *Southern Recorder*, January 17, 1833.
[21] *Niles's Register*, XLIV, 202 and 359.
[22] *Niles's Register*, XLVII, 190. Georgia Senate *Journal*, 1830, p. 139. Acts of Georgia General Assembly, 1834, p. 337.

government in Georgia and Alabama would not be countenanced by the President. During 1829 and 1830 his agents were urging the Cherokee chiefs to make a cession and at the same time persuading individual tribesmen to move west. In the latter year he threw open the lands vacated by the piecemeal removal for disposition by Georgia, but ordered a stop to the removal of the Cherokees in small parties with the purpose of building up a strong cession party within the tribe east of the Mississippi.[23]

The State government was not unmindful of its advantageous position. In 1831 the legislature directed the governor to have all the unceded territory in the State surveyed, and to distribute the land among the citizens of the State by the land-lottery system. An act of December, 1834, authorized the immediate occupation of the lands thus allotted, though it gave the Indians two years in which to remove from their individual holdings.[24]

President Jackson persisted in his attempts to persuade the Cherokees to remove in a body. Early in 1834 it was discovered that a treaty party was developing in the nation. This party sent a delegation to Washington, which signed a preliminary treaty looking to a cession, but John Ross, the principal chief of the nation, protested, May 29, 1834, with such a show of support by the great bulk of the nation that the treaty failed of ratification.[25]

The division among the Cherokee leaders had at length opened a way for the final success of Georgia's efforts. In February, 1835, two rival Cherokee delegations appeared at Washington, with John Ross at the head of the orthodox party and John Ridge as the leader of the faction in favor of emigration. John Ridge, Major Ridge, Elias Boudinot, and other chiefs had finally come to see the futility of opposition to the inevitable, and were ready to lead their people westward. The Ridge party signed a treaty of cession on March 14, which required the approval of the whole Cherokee Nation before becoming effective; but in a council of the Cherokees, held at Running Waters in June, Ross succeeded in having the treaty rejected.[26]

The maneuvering of the two factions in the following months engendered ill-feeling among the Cherokees and strengthened the position of Georgia. In December, 1835, a council was called by United States commissioners to meet at New Echota. The meeting was a small one, because of the opposition of the Ross party; but on December 29 a treaty was signed with the chiefs attending which provided for the cession of all the remaining Cherokee lands east of the Mississippi River for $5,000,-000 and lands in the West. The Ross party protested against the treaty, but were not able to prevent its ratification at Washington.[27]

The news of the definitive ratification served only to increase the discontent among the Indians. A confidential agent of the Secretary of War reported, September 25, 1837, that upon investigation he found that the whole

[23] *Athenian*, December 22, 1829. Message of Governor Gilmer, *Niles's Register*, XXXIX, 339. Royce, *The Cherokee Nation*, p. 261.
[24] Acts of Ga. Gen. Assem., 1831, p. 141. Acts of Ga. Gen. Assem., 1834, p. 105. Prince, *Digest of Georgia Laws to 1837*, p. 262.
[25] Royce, *The Cherokee Nation*, p. 275.

[26] White, *Historical Collections of Georgia*, p. 143. Royce, *The Cherokee Nation*, p. 279. *Southern Banner*, Apr. 16 and June 18, 1835.
[27] Acts of Ga. Gen. Assem., 1835, p. 342. *Niles's Register*, XLIX, 343.

Cherokee Nation was irreconcilable to the treaty and determined that it should not bind them.[28]

Public sentiment throughout the United States, especially among the opponents of the Administration, became deeply stirred with sympathy for the Indians. Within the halls of Congress Webster, Clay, and Calhoun were vigorous in their condemnation of the New Echota treaty.[29] President Van Buren was so influenced by this torrent of remonstrance and criticism as to suggest to the governors of Georgia, Alabama, Tennessee, and North Carolina, on May 23, 1838, that an extension of not more than two years be allowed in which the Cherokees might move away. Mr. Gilmer, who had again become governor of

Georgia, replied, on May 28, that he could give the plan no sanction whatever. He feared that the suggestion was the beginning of another attack upon the sovereignty of the State, and declared his determination to take charge of the removal in person if the Federal Government should fail in its duty.[30]

There was, however, to be no further contest. General Scott had already arrived in the Cherokee country to direct the removal. He issued a proclamation, May 10, 1838, that every Cherokee man, woman, and child must be on their way west within a month. On May 18 John Ross made a last ineffectual offer to arrange a substitute treaty. The emigration was at once pushed forward, and on December 4 the last party of the Cherokees took up their westward march.

[28] Royce, *The Cherokee Nation*, p. 286.
[29] Benton, *Thirty Years' View*, I, 625. Royce, *The Cherokee Nation*, p. 290.
[30] Gilmer, *Georgians*, pp. 240 and 538.

Andrew Jackson:

THE CONDITION AND ULTERIOR DESTINY OF THE INDIAN TRIBES (DECEMBER 8, 1829)

*We speak often of "Jacksonian" America, and in so doing we ac-
knowledge the hero of the Battle of New Orleans as one of the most
important leaders of his time. Andrew Jackson was, as John William
Ward has suggested in a book on the subject, a symbol even to his
contemporaries.*[1] *Old Hickory entered the White House as the cham-
pion of the "common man." His eviction of the learned and scholarly
John Quincy Adams meant, to mournful New Englanders and to
jubilant frontiersmen, that the West had come of age. It meant also
a new impetus to the drive for the removal of the Indians then dwelling within the borders of the States. Jackson argued that he was fur-
thering traditional policies, but his emphases and his attitudes reveal
discontinuities as well as continuities. It was, moreover, not easy to
say just what these traditional policies were.*

*Although the Continental Congress had recognized the importance
of Indian policy and had, by the Act of July 12, 1775, divided the
country into "departments" and appointed "commissioners," our national policy was first set forth by Henry Knox, George Washington's
Secretary of War. Knox, in a message to the president, urged that
Congress purchase western lands from the Indians and remove the
tribes before allotting the lands to settlers.*[2] *From Washington's administration to Jackson's, American presidents followed this course.
Knox had also argued that, "instead of exterminating a part of the
human race," we should have devoted ourselves to imparting "our
knowledge of cultivation and the arts to the aboriginals of the country. . . ."*[3] *Thomas Jefferson spoke in his first Annual Message of "the
continued efforts to introduce among [the Indians] the implements and
the practice of husbandry and of the household arts . . . ,"*[4] *and Jef-*

[1] See John William Ward, *Andrew Jackson: Symbol for an Age* (New York:
Oxford University Press, 1955).
[2] *American State Papers:* Indian Affairs, I, 52–54.
[3] *Ibid.,* p. 53.
[4] J. D. Richardson, ed., *Compilation of the Messages and Papers of the Presidents: 1789–1897,* I, 326.

ferson, in a message to Congress (January 18, 1803), advocated the teaching of agricultural techniques and the establishing of trading houses as a way of civilizing the Indians and, thereby, of increasing their readiness to cede their lands: "In leading them . . . to agriculture, to manufactures, and civilization; in bringing together their and our sentiments, and in preparing them ultimately to participate in the benefits of our Government, I trust and believe we are acting for their greatest good."⁵ As the Indians progessed in the arts of civilization, it became apparent that the goals outlined by General Knox might prove to be contradictory. Specifically, as the Creeks and Cherokees became civilized, they became more determined in their desire to hold their lands and to prevent the intrusion of white settlers. Georgia, fearing that the Indians would never agree to peaceable removal, asked President Monroe to remove the Indians by force. He refused.⁶ Two years later, in 1825, Governor Troup of Georgia attempted to survey lands recently ceded by the Creeks, only to have President Adams question the validity of the Treaty of Indian Springs (February 12, 1825). When Adams attempted to halt the surveying, Troup ordered the citizens of Georgia to prepare for an armed clash; only the willingness of the Creeks to negotiate a new treaty prevented immediate bloodshed.⁷

Meanwhile, the Cherokee nation had progressed far enough to proclaim itself a republic and to ratify a constitution modeled on that of the United States (July, 1827). As Georgia grew less and less patient, the policy of Indian "improvement" seemed to be defeating the policy of Indian removal. Then, in rapid succession, came the election to the presidency of Andrew Jackson (November, 1828), the extension of Georgia' law over all white persons in the Cherokee territory (December, 1828), and the discovery of gold in the Cherokee territory (July, 1829). The Georgians assumed that Jackson, himself a frontiersman and an Indian fighter, would help them in their efforts to coerce the Cherokees into removal. Any doubts which the Georgians might have had were dispelled by Jackson's first Annual Message.

T HE condition and ulterior destiny of the Indian tribes within the limits of some of our States have become ob-

⁵ *Ibid.*, p. 352.
⁶ See George D. Harmon, *Sixty Years of Indian Affairs* (Chapel Hill: University of North Carolina Press, 1941), pp. 173–174.
⁷ For relevant documents, see *American State Papers: Indian Affairs*, II, 727–872.

jects of much interest and importance. It has long been the policy of Government to introduce among them the arts of civilization, in the hope of gradually reclaiming them from a wandering life. This policy has, however, been coupled with another wholly incompatible with its success. Professing a desire to civilize

Andrew Jackson, "The Condition & Ulterior Destiny of the Indian Tribes," from First Annual Message, J. D. Richardson, ed., *A Compilation of the Messages & Papers of the Presidents: 1789–1897*, II, 456–459.

and settle them, we have at the same time lost no opportunity to purchase their lands and thrust them farther into the wilderness. By this means they have not only been kept in a wandering state, but been led to look upon us as unjust and indifferent to their fate. Thus, though lavish in its expenditures upon the subject, Government has constantly defeated its own policy, and the Indians in general, receding farther and farther to the west, have retained their savage habits. A portion, however, of the Southern tribes, having mingled much with the whites and made some progress in the arts of civilized life, have lately attempted to erect an independent government within the limits of Georgia and Alabama. These States, claiming to be the only sovereigns within their territories, extended their laws over the Indians, which induced the latter to call upon the United States for protection.

Under these circumstances the question presented was whether the General Government had a right to sustain those people in their pretensions. The Constitution declares that "no new State shall be formed or erected within the jurisdiction of any other State" without the consent of its legislature. If the General Government is not permitted to tolerate the erection of a confederate State within the territory of one of the members of this Union against her consent, much less could it allow a foreign and independent government to establish itself there. Georgia became a member of the Confederacy which eventuated in our Federal Union as a sovereign State, always asserting her claim to certain limits, which, having been originally defined in her colonial charter and subsequently recognized in the treaty of peace, she has ever since continued to enjoy, except as they have been circum-scribed by her own voluntary transfer of a portion of her territory to the United States in the articles of cession of 1802. Alabama was admitted into the Union on the same footing with the original States, with boundaries which were prescribed by Congress. There is no constitutional, conventional, or legal provision which allows them less power over the Indians within their borders than is possessed by Maine or New York. Would the people of Maine permit the Penobscot tribe to erect an independent government within their State? And unless they did would it not be the duty of the General Government to support them in resisting such a measure? Would the people of New York permit each remnant of the Six Nations within her borders to declare itself an independent people under the protection of the United States? Could the Indians establish a separate republic on each of their reservations in Ohio? And if they were so disposed would it be the duty of this Government to protect them in the attempt? If the principle involved in the obvious answer to these questions be abandoned, it will follow that the objects of this Government are reversed, and that it has become a part of its duty to aid in destroying the States which it was established to protect.

Actuated by this view of the subject, I informed the Indians inhabiting parts of Georgia and Alabama that their attempt to establish an independent government would not be countenanced by the Executive of the United States, and advised them to emigrate beyond the Mississippi or submit to the laws of those States.

Our conduct toward these people is deeply interesting to our national character. Their present condition, contrasted with what they once were, makes a most powerful appeal to our sympathies. Our ancestors found them the uncontrolled possessors of these vast regions. By persuasion and force they have been made to retire from river to river and from mountain to mountain, until some of the tribes have become extinct and others have left but remnants to preserve for a while their once terrible names. Surrounded by the whites with their arts of civilization, which by destroying the resources of the savage doom him to weakness and decay, the fate of the Mohegan, the Narragansett, and the Delaware is fast overtaking the Choctaw, the Cherokee, and the Creek. That this fate surely awaits them if they remain within the limits of the States does not admit of a doubt. Humanity and national honor demand that every effort should be made to avert so great a calamity. It is too late to inquire whether it was just in the United States to include them and their territory within the bounds of new States, whose limits they could control. That step can not be retraced. A State can not be dismembered by Congress or restricted in the exercise of her constitutional power. But the people of those States and of every State, actuated by feelings of justice and a regard for our national honor, submit to you the interesting question whether something can not be done, consistently with the rights of the States, to preserve this much-injured race.

As a means of effecting this end I suggest for your consideration the propriety of setting apart an ample district west of the Mississippi, and without the limits of any State or Territory now formed, to be guaranteed to the Indian tribes as long as they shall occupy it, each tribe having a distinct control over the portion designated for its use. There they may be secured in the enjoyment of governments of their own choice, subject to no other control from the United States than such as may be necessary to preserve peace on the frontier and between the several tribes. There the benevolent may endeavor to teach them the arts of civilization, and, by promoting union and harmony among them, to raise up an interesting commonwealth, destined to perpetuate the race and to attest the humanity and justice of this Government.

This emigration should be voluntary, for it would be as cruel as unjust to compel the aborigines to abandon the graves of their fathers and seek a home in a distant land. But they should be distinctly informed that if they remain within the limits of the States they must be subject to their laws. In return for their obedience as individuals they will without doubt be protected in the enjoyment of those possessions which they have improved by their industry. But it seems to me visionary to suppose that in this state of things claims can be allowed on tracts of country on which they have neither dwelt nor made improvements, merely because they have seen them from the mountain or passed them in the chase. Submitting to the laws of the States, and receiving, like other citizens, protection in their persons and property, they will ere long become merged in the mass of our population.

LAND POLICIES AND THE GEORGIA
LAW OF DECEMBER 19, 1829

The Federal Government's land policy had been a democratic one in that the Ordinance of 1785 specified that lands purchased from the Indians were to be surveyed and sold at auction in lots of not less than 640 acres and at a minimum price of $1 an acre. Unfortunately, these apparently liberal terms gave speculators advantages over farmers, few of whom had funds sufficient to purchase 640 acres and, at the same time, to establish themselves on their newly purchased lands. By 1832, federal lands were sold in lots of 40 acres at a minimum auction price of $1.25 an acre, but even this liberalization of land policy was illiberal compared to the system established in Georgia.[1] Georgia's Act of May 11, 1803, provided for a centrally administered system by which lands were distributed through lotteries in which everyone had, substantially, an equal chance. Lands were priced from six and a half cents to one dollar an acre. Under this policy, despite speculation and fraud, three-fourths of the area of the state was parcelled out to 100,-000 individuals at an average price of approximately ten cents an acre, far less than 10% of the price of federal lands. The land lotteries of 1821 and of 1827 disposed of the lands ceded by the Creek nation. In 1828 and 1829, the people of Georgia looked for fresh lands and, while looking, sang these revealing lyrics: "All I ask in this creation / Is a pretty little wife and a big plantation / Way up yonder in the Cherokee Nation."

Georgia lost little time pondering President Jackson's Annual Message. On December 19, 1829, Governor George R. Gilmer signed into law a bill which, in effect, gave the Cherokees less than seven months to conclude their affairs as a semi-autonomous nation. The people of Georgia expected that the Cherokee lands would soon be distributed by the lottery system. (Their expectations were met in 1832, when, three years before the final cession of the lands by the Cherokees, the territory was surveyed and allotted to the people of Georgia.) In signing the law herein reprinted, Governor Gilmer, who was not a

---

[1] For Federal land policy, see Roy M. Robbins, *Our Landed Heritage* (Princeton: Princeton University Press, 1942); for Georgia's policy, see Milton S. Heath, *Constructive Liberalism: The Role of the State in Economic Development in Georgia to 1860* (Cambridge: Harvard University Press, 1954), pp. 139–158.

*member of either of the two major factions in Georgia politics, was
carrying out the fervent wishes of both the "Lumpkin men" and the
"Troup men."*[2]

BE it enacted by the senate and house of representatives of the state of Georgia in general assembly met, and it is hereby enacted by the authority of the same, That from and after the passing of this act, all that part of the unlocated territory within the limits of this state, and which lies between the Alabama line and the old path leading from the Buzzard Roost on the Chattahoochie to Sally Hughes', on the Hightower river, thence to Thomas Petets, on the old federal road: thence with said road to the Alabama line, be, and the same is hereby added to, and shall become a part of the county of Carroll.

Sec. 2. And be it further enacted, That all that part of said territory lying and being north of the last mentioned line, and south of the road running from Charles Gates' ferry, on the Chattahoochie river, to Dick Roe's, to where it intersects with the path aforesaid, be, and the same is hereby added to, and shall become a part of the county of DeKalb.

Sec. 3. And be it further enacted, That all that part of said territory lying north of the last mentioned line, and south of a line commencing at the mouth of Baldridge's creek: thence up said creek to its source: from thence to where the Federal road crosses the Hightower: thence with said road to the Tennessee line, be, and the same is hereby added to, and

shall become a part of the county of Gwinnett.

Sec. 4. And be it further enacted, That all that part of said territory lying north of said last mentioned line and south of a line to commence on the Chestatee river at the mouth of Yoholo creek: thence up said creek to the top of the Blue ridge: thence to the head waters of Notley river: thence down said river to the boundary line of Georgia, be, and the same is hereby added to, and shall become a part of the county of Hall.

Sec. 5. And be it further enacted, That all that part of said territory, lying north of said last mentioned line, within the limits of this state, be, and the same is hereby added to, and shall become a part of the county of Habersham.

Sec. 6. And be it further enacted, That all the laws, both civil and criminal of this state, be, and the same are hereby extended over said portions of territory respectively, and all persons whatever, residing within the same, shall, after the first day of June next, be subject and liable to the operation of said laws, in the same manner as other citizens of this state, or the citizens of said counties respectively, and all writs and processes whatever issued by the courts or officers of said courts, shall extend over, and operate on the portions of territory hereby added to the same respectively.

Sec. 7. And be it further enacted, That after the first day of June next, all laws, ordinances, orders and regulations of any kind whatever, made, passed, or enacted by the Cherokee Indians, either in general council or in any other way what-

2 For brief comments on the two factions, see headnotes to selections from Lumpkin and from Troup. For extended analyses of state politics, see Phillips, *Georgia and State Rights*, pp. 113–143; and Paul Murray, *The Whig Party in Georgia* (Chapel Hill: University of North Carolina Press, 1948).

"Georgia and the Indians." From *Niles's Weekly Register*, XXXVIII (March 13, 1830), 54–55.

ever, or by any authority whatever of said tribe, be, and the same are hereby declared to be null and void and of no effect, as if the same had never existed; and in all cases of indictment or civil suits, it shall not be lawful for the defendant to justify under any of said laws, ordinances, orders, or regulations; nor shall the courts of this state permit the same to be given in evidence on the trial of any suit whatever.

Sec. 8. And be it further enacted, That it shall not be lawful for any person or body of persons by arbitrary power or by virtue of any pretended rule, ordinance, law, or custom of said Cherokee nation, to prevent, by threats, menaces, or other means, to endeavor to prevent any Indian of said nation residing within the chartered limits of this state, from enrolling as an emigrant or actually emigrating, or removing from said nation; nor shall it be lawful for any person or body of persons by arbitrary power or by virtue of any pretended rule, ordinance, law, or custom of said nation, to punish in any manner, or to molest either the person or property, or to abridge the rights or privileges of any Indian for enrolling his or her name as an emigrant, or for emigrating, or intending to emigrate from said nation.

Sec. 9. And be it further enacted, That any person or body of persons offending against the provisions of the foregoing section, shall be guilty of a high misdemeanor, subject to indictment, and on conviction, shall be punished by confinement in the common jail of any county of this state, or by confinement at hard labor in the penitentiary for a term not exceeding four years, at the discretion of the court.

Sec. 10. And be it further enacted, That it shall not be lawful for any person or body of persons, by arbitrary power, or under color of any pretended rule, ordinance, law, or custom of said nation to prevent, or offer to prevent, or deter any Indian, head man, chief, or warrior of said nation residing within the chartered limits of this state, from selling or ceding to the United States, for the use of Georgia, the whole or any part of said territory, or to prevent, or offer to prevent any Indian, head man, chief or warrior of said nation, residing as aforesaid, from meeting in council or treaty, any commissioner or commissioners on the part of the United States, for any purpose whatever.

Sec. 11. And be it further enacted, That any person or body of persons, offending against the provisions of the foregoing section, shall be guilty of a high misdemeanor, subject to indictment, and on conviction, shall be confined at hard labor in the penetentiary, for not less than four, nor longer than six years, at the discretion of the court.

Sec. 12. And be it further enacted, That it shall not be lawful for any person or body of persons by arbitrary force, or under color of any pretended rules, ordinances, law, or custom of said nation, to take the life of any Indian residing as aforesaid for enlisting as an emigrant, attempting to emigrate, ceding or attempting to cede as aforesaid, the whole or part of said territory, or meeting or attempting to meet in treaty or in council as aforesaid, any commissioner or commissioners as aforesaid; and any persons or body of persons, offending against the provisions of this section, shall be guilty of murder, subject to indictment, and on conviction shall suffer death by hanging.

Sec. 13. And be it further enacted, That should any of the foregoing offences be committed under color of any pretended rules, ordinance, custom or law of said nation, all persons acting therein either as individuals or as pretended executive, ministerial, or judicial officers, shall be deemed and considered as principals, and subject to the pains and penalties herein before prescribed.

Sec. 14. And be it further enacted, That for all demands which may come within the jurisdiction of a magistrate's court, suit may be brought for the same in the nearest district of the county to which the territory is hereby annexed, and all officers serving any legal process, or any person living on any portion of the territory herein named, shall be entitled to receive the sum of five cents for every mile he may ride to serve the same, after crossing the present limits of said counties, in addition to the fees already allowed by law; and in case any of said officers should be resisted in the execution of any legal process issued by any court or magistrate, justice of the inferior court or judge of the superior court of any of said counties, he is hereby authorised to call out a sufficient number of the militia of said counties to aid and protect him in the execution of his duty.

Sec. 15. And be it further enacted, That no Indian or descendant of any Indian, residing within the Creek or Cherokee nations of Indians, shall be deemed a competent witness in any court of this state to which a white person may be a party, except such white person resides within the said nation.

WARREN JOURDAN,
speaker of the house of representatives.

THOMAS STOCKS,
president of the senate.

Assented to, Dec. 19, 1829.

GEORGE R. GILMER, governor.

Senator Theodore Frelinghuysen:
SPEECH BEFORE THE SENATE
(APRIL 9, 1830)

Legislation such as the Georgia Law of December 19, 1829, repre-
sented one threat to the survival of the Cherokee nation. Even as the
Georgia legislature acted, Wilson Lumpkin, Georgia's representative
on the House Committee on Indian Affairs, worked to secure national
legislation further implementing the policy of Indian removal. A bill,
reported to the House on February 24, 1830, specified that the presi-
dent be authorized "to exchange the public domain in the West for
Indian lands in the East, to give perpetual title to the country thus
exchanged, to pay for improvements made upon the old possessions,
and to give aid and assistance in emigration. The measure was not to
interfere with existing treaties and the sum of $500,000 was [to be]
appropriated for the purpose of making removal possible."[1] This bill
brought forth protracted and vehement debate in both houses of Con-
gress. The most notable speech made was that of New Jersey's Senator
Frelinghuysen, then serving his only term in the Senate. Frelinghuysen
spoke for six hours, over a period of three days, and became nationally
famous. On the basis of this speech against Indian removal, Freling-
huysen was denominated, in a poem by the abolitionist William Lloyd
Garrison, "patriot and Christian." The name stuck. Frelinghuysen, who
went on to become president of the American Bible Society, chancel-
lor of New York University, vice-presidential candidate of the Whigs
in 1844, and, finally, president of Rutgers College, was known for the
rest of his life as the "Christian statesman."

GOD, in his providence, planted these tribes on this western continent, so far as we know, before Great Britain herself had a political existence. I believe, Sir, it is not now seriously denied that the Indians are men, endowed with kindred faculties and powers with our- selves; that they have a place in human sympathy, and are justly entitled to a share in the common bounties of a benig- nant Providence. And, with this con- ceded, I ask in what code of the law of nations, or by what process of abstract deduction, their rights have been ex- tinguished?

[1] Harmon, *Sixty Years of Indian Affairs*, p. 175.

From Gales & Seaton's *Register of Debates in Congress*, VI, Part 1, 311–316.

Where is the decree or ordinance, that has stripped these early and first lords of the soil? Sir, no record of such measure can be found. And I might triumphantly rest the hopes of these feeble fragments of once great nations upon this impregnable foundation. However mere human policy, or the law of power, or the tyrant's plea of expediency, may have found it convenient at any or in all times to recede from the unchangeable principles of eternal justice, no argument can shake the political maxim, that, where the Indian always has been, he enjoys an absolute right still to be, in the free exercise of his own modes of thought, government and conduct.

In the light of natural law, can a reason for a distinction exist in the mode of enjoying that which is my own? If I use land for hunting, may another take it because he needs it for agriculture? I am aware that some writers have, by a system of artificial reasoning, endeavored to justify, or rather excuse the encroachments made upon Indian territory; and they denominate these abstractions the law of nations, and, in this ready way, the question is despatched. Sir, as we trace the sources of this law, we find its authority to depend either upon the conventions or common consent of nations. And when, permit me to inquire, were the Indian tribes ever consulted on the establishment of such a law? Whoever represented them or their interests in any congress of nations, to confer upon the public rules of intercourse, and the proper foundations of dominion and property? The plain matter of fact is, that all these partial doctrines have resulted from the selfish plans and pursuits of more enlightened nations; and it is not matter for any great wonder, that they should so largely partake of a mercenary and exclusive spirit toward the claims of the Indians.

It is, however, admitted, Sir, that, when the increase of population and the wants of mankind demand the cultivation of the earth, a duty is thereby devolved upon the proprietors of large and uncultivated regions, of devoting them to such useful purposes. But such appropriations are to be obtained by fair contract, and for reasonable compensation. It is, in such a case, the duty of the proprietor to sell: we may properly address his reason to induce him; but we cannot rightfully compel the cession of his lands, or take them by violence, if his consent be withheld.

It is with great satisfaction that I am enabled, upon the best authority, to affirm, that this duty has been largely and generously met and fulfilled on the part of the aboriginal proprietors of this continent. Several years ago, official reports to Congress stated the amount of Indian grants to the United States to exceed 214 millions of acres. Yes, sir, we have acquired, and now own more land as the fruits of their bounty than we shall dispose of at the present rate to actual settlers in two hundred years. For, very recently, it has been ascertained, on this floor, that our public sales average not more than about one million of acres annually. It greatly aggravates the wrong that is now meditated against these tribes, the rich and ample districts of their territories, that either force or persuasion have incorporated into our public domains. As the tide of our population has rolled on, we have added purchase to purchase. The confiding Indian listened to our professions of friendship: we called him brother, and he believed us. Millions after millions he has yielded to our importunity, until we have acquired more than can be cultivated in centuries—and yet we crave more. We have crowded the tribes upon a few miserable acres on our southern frontier: it is all that is left to them of their once boundless forests: and still, like the horse-leech, our insatiated cupidity cries, give! give!

Before I proceed to deduce collateral confirmations of this original title, from all our political intercourse and conventions with the Indian tribes, I beg leave to pause a moment, and view the case as it lies beyond the treaties made with them; and aside also from all conflicting claims between the confederation, and the colonies, and the Congress of the States. Our ancestors found these people, far removed from the commotions of Europe, exercising all the rights, and enjoying the privileges, of free and independent sovereigns of this new world. They were not a wild and lawless horde of banditti, but lived under the restraints of government, patriarchal in its character, and energetic in its influence. They had chiefs, head men, and councils. The white men, the authors of all their wrongs, approached them as friends— they extended the olive branch; and, being then a feeble colony and at the mercy of the native tenants of the soil, by presents and professions, propitiated their good will. The Indian yielded a slow, but substantial confidence; granted to the colonists an abiding place; and suffered them to grow up to man's estate beside him. He never raised the claim of elder title. As the white man's wants increased, he opened the hand of his bounty wider and wider. By and by, conditions are changed. His people melt away; his lands are constantly coveted; millions after millions are ceded. The Indian bears it all meekly; he complains, indeed, as well he may; but suffers on: and now he finds that this neighbor,

whom his kindness had nourished, has spread an adverse title over the last remains of his patrimony, barely adequate to his wants, and turns upon him, and says, "away! we cannot endure you so near us! These forests and rivers, these groves of your fathers, these firesides and hunting grounds, are ours by the right of power, and the force of numbers."

Sir, let every treaty be blotted from our records, and in the judgment of natural and unchangeable truth and justice, I ask, who is the injured, and who is the aggressor? Let conscience answer, and I fear not the result. Sir, let those who please, denounce the public feeling on this subject as the morbid excitement of a false humanity; but I return with the inquiry, whether I have not presented the case truly, with no feature of it overcharged or distorted? And, in view of it, who can help feeling, Sir? Do the obligations of justice change with the color of the skin? Is it one of the prerogatives of the white man, that he may disregard the dictates of moral principles, when an Indian shall be concerned? No, Sir. In that severe and impartial scrutiny, which futurity will cast over this subject, the righteous award will be, that those very causes which are now pleaded for the relaxed enforcement of the rules of equity, urged upon us not only a rigid execution of the highest justice, to the very letter, but claimed at our hands a generous and magnanimous policy.

Standing here, then, on this unshaken basis, how is it possible that even a shadow of claim to soil, or jurisdiction, can be derived, by forming a collateral issue between the State of Georgia and the general government? Her complaint is made against the United States, for encroachments on her sovereignty. Sir, the Cherokees are no parties to this issue;

they have no part in this controversy. They hold by better title than either Georgia or the Union. They have nothing to do with State sovereignty, or United States, sovereignty. They are above and beyond both. True, Sir, they have made treaties with both, but not to acquire title or jurisdiction; these they had before—ages before the evil hour, to them, when their white brothers fled to them for an asylum. They treated to secure protection and guaranty for subsisting powers and privileges; and so far as those conventions raise obligations, they are willing to meet, and always have met, and faithfully performed them; and now expect from a great people the like fidelity to plighted covenants.

I have thus endeavored to bring this question up to the control of first principles. I forget all that we have promised, and all that Georgia has repeatedly conceded, and, by her conduct, confirmed. Sir, in this abstract presentation of the case, stripped of every collateral circumstance—and these only the more firmly established the Indian claims— thus regarded, if the contending parties were to exchange positions; place the white man where the Indian stands; load him with all these wrongs, and what path would his outraged feelings strike out for his career? Twenty shillings tax, I think it was, imposed upon the immortal Hampden, roused into activity the slumbering fires of liberty in the Old World, from which she dates a glorious epoch, whose healthful influence still cherishes the spirit of freedom. A few pence of duty on tea, that invaded no fireside, excited no fears, disturbed no substantial interest whatever, awakened in the American colonies a spirit of firm resistance; and how was the tea tax met, Sir? Just as it should be. There was lurking beneath this trifling imposition of duty, a covert assumption of authority, that led directly to oppressive exactions. "No taxation without representation," became our motto. We would neither pay the tax nor drink the tea. Our fathers buckled on their armor, and, from the water's edge, repelled the encroachments of a misguided cabinet. We successfully and triumphantly contended for the very rights and privileges that our Indian neighbors now implore us to protect and preserve to them. Sir, this thought invests the subject under debate with most singular and momentous interest. *We,* whom God has exalted to the very summit of prosperity—whose brief career forms the brightest page in history; the wonder and praise of the world; Freedom's hope, and her consolation; about to turn traitors to our principles and our fame—about to become the oppressors of the feeble, and to cast away our birthright! Sir, I hope for better things.

It is a subject full of grateful satisfaction, that, in our public intercourse with the Indians, ever since the first colonies of white men found an abode on these Western shores, we have distinctly recognised their title; treated with them as owners, and in all our acquisitions of territory, applied ourselves to these ancient proprietors, by purchase and cession alone, to obtain the right of soil. Sir, I challenge the record of any other or different pretension. When, or where, did any assembly or convention meet which proclaimed, or even suggested to these tribes, that the right of discovery contained a superior efficacy over all prior titles?

And our recognition was not confined to the soil merely. We regarded them as nations—far behind us indeed in civilization, but still we respected their forms of government—we conformed our conduct to their notions of civil policy. We were aware of the potency of any edict that sprang from the deliberations of the council fire; and when we desired lands, or peace, or alliances, to this source of power and energy, to this great lever of Indian government we addressed our proposals—to this alone did we look; and from this alone did we expect aid or relief. . . .

Under the confederation of the old Thirteen States, and shortly before the adoption of the Constitution, on the 20th of November, 1785, a treaty was made with the Cherokee nation at Hopewell. This treaty, according to its title, was concluded between "Commissioners Plenipotentiary of the United States of America, of the one part, and the Headmen and Warriors of all the Cherokees, of the other." It gives "peace to all the Cherokees," and receives them into the favor and protection of the United States. And, by the first article, the Cherokees agree to restore all the prisoners, citizens of the United States, or subjects of their allies, to their entire liberty. Here, again, we discover the same magnanimous policy of renouncing any pretended rights of a conqueror in our negotiations with the allies of our enemy. We invite them to peace; we engage to become their protectors, and in the stipulation for the liberation of prisoners, we trace again the broad line of distinction between citizens of the United States and the Cherokee people.

Who, after this, sir, can retain a single doubt as to the unquestioned political sovereignty of these tribes? It is very true, that they were not absolutely independent. As they had become comparatively feeble, and as they were, in the mass, an uncivilized race, they chose to depend upon us for protection; but this did not destroy or affect their sovereignty. The rule of public law is clearly stated by Vattel—"one community may be bound to another by a very unequal alliance, and still be a sovereign State. Though a weak State, in order to provide for its safety, should place itself under the protection of a more powerful one, yet, if it reserves to itself the right of governing its own body, it ought to be considered as an independent State." If the right of self-government is retained, the State preserves its political existence; and, permit me to ask, when did the Southern Indians relinquish of this right? Sir, they have always exercised it, and were never disturbed in the enjoyment of it, until the late legislation of Georgia and the States of Alabama and Mississippi.

The treaty next proceeds to establish territorial domains and to forbid all intrusions upon the Cherokee country, by any of our citizens, on the pains of outlawry. It provides, that, if any citizen of the United States shall remain on the lands of the Indians for six months "after the ratification of the treaty, such person shall forfeit the protection of the United States, and the Indians may punish him, or not, as they please." What stronger attribute of sovereignty could have been conceded to this tribe, than to have accorded to them the power of punishing our citizens according to their own laws and modes; and, sir, what more satisfactory proof can be furnished to the Senate, of the sincere and inflexible purpose of the Government to maintain the rights of the Indian nations, than the annexation of such sanctions as the forfeiture of national protection, and the infliction upon intruders of any punishment within the range of savage discretion? It is to be recollected, that this treaty was made at a time when all admit the Cherokees to have been, with very rare exceptions, in the rudest state of Pagan darkness. . . .

The next important event, in connexion with the Cherokees, is the treaty of Holston, made with them on the 2d July, 1791. This was the first treaty negotiated with the Cherokees after the constitution. And it is only necessary to consider the import of its preamble, to become satisfied of the constancy of our policy, in adhering to the first principles of our Indian negotiations. Sir, let it be remembered that this was a crisis when the true spirit of the constitution would be best understood; most of those who framed it came into the councils of the country in 1789. Let it be well pondered, that this treaty of Holston was the public compact in which General Washington, as a preparative solemnity, asked the advice of the Senate, and concerning which, he inquired of that venerable body, whether, in the treaty to be made, the United States should solemnly guaranty the new boundary, to be ascertained and fixed between them and the Cherokees.

The preamble to this treaty I will now recite:

"The parties being desirous of establishing permanent peace and friendship between the United States and the said Cherokee nation, and the citizens and members thereof, and to remove the causes of war, by ascertaining their limits, and making other necessary, just, and friendly arrangements: the President of the United States, by William Blount, Governor of the territory of the United States of America, South of the river Ohio, and superintendent of Indian affairs for the Southern District, who is vested with full powers for these purposes, by and with the advice and consent of the Senate of the United States; and the Cherokee nation, by the undersigned chiefs and warriors representing the said nation, have agreed to the following articles," &c.

The first article stipulates that there shall be "perpetual peace and friendship" between the parties; a subsequent article provides, that the boundary between the United States and the Cherokees "shall be ascertained and marked plainly, by three persons appointed by the United States, and three Cherokees on the part of their nation."

In pursuance of the advice of the Senate, by the 7th article of this treaty, "The United States solemnly guaranty to the Cherokee nation all their lands not hereby ceded."

And after several material clauses, the concluding article suspends the effect and obligation of the treaty upon its ratification "by the President of the United States, with the advice and consent of the Senate of the United States."

Now, sir, it is a most striking part of this history, that every possible incident, of form, deliberation, advisement, and power, attended this compact. The Senate was consulted when our plenipotentiary was commissioned; full powers were then given to our commissioner; the articles were agreed upon; the treaty referred to the Executive and Senate for their ratification, and, with all its provisions, by them solemnly confirmed.

It requires a fulness of self-respect and self-confidence, the lot of a rare few, after time has added its sanctions to this high pledge of national honor, to attempt to convict the illustrious men of that Senate of gross ignorance of constitutional power; to charge against them that they strangely mistook the charter under which they acted; and violated almost the proprieties of language, as some gentlemen contend, by dignifying with the name and formalities of a treaty "mere bargains to get Indian lands." Sir, who so well understood the nature and extent of the powers granted in the Constitution, as the statesmen who aided by their personal counsels to establish it?

Every administration of this Government, from President Washington's, have, with like solemnities and stipulations, held treaties with the Cherokees; treaties, too, by almost all of which we obtained further acquisitions of their territory. Yes, sir, whenever we approached them in the language of friendship and kindness, we touched the chord that won their confidence; and now, when they have nothing left with which to satisfy our cravings, we propose to annul every treaty—to gainsay our word— and, by violence and perfidy, drive the Indian from his home. In a subsequent treaty between the United States and the Cherokee nation, concluded on the 8th July, 1817, express reference is made to past negotiations between the parties, on the subject of removal to the west of the Mississippi; the same question that now agitates the country, and engages our deliberations. And this convention is deserving of particular notice, inasmuch as we learn from it, not only what sentiments were then entertained by our government towards the Cherokees, but, also, in what light the different dispositions of the Indians to emigrate to the West, and to remain on their [ancient] patrimony, were considered. This treaty recites that application had been made to the United States, at a previous period, by a deputation of the Cherokees [on the 9th of January, 1809], by which they apprized the government of the wish of a part of their nation to remove west of the Mississippi, and of

the residue to abide in their old habitations. That the President of the United States, after maturely considering the subject, answered the petition as follows: "The United States, my children, are the friends of both parties, and, as far as can be reasonably asked, they are willing to satisfy the wishes of both. Those who remain may be assured of our patronage, our aid, and our good neighborhood." "To those who remove, every aid shall be administered, and when established at their new settlements, we shall consider them as our children, and always hold them firmly by the hand." The convention then establishes new boundaries and pledges our faith to respect and defend the Indian territories. Some matters, by universal consent, are taken as granted, without any explicit recognition. Under the influence of this rule of common fairness, how can we ever dispute the sovereign right of the Cherokees to remain east of the Mississippi, when it was in relation to that very location, that we promised our patronage, aid, and good neighborhood? Sir, is this high-handed encroachment of Georgia to be the commentary upon the national pledge here given, and the obvious import of these terms? How were these people to remain, if not as they then existed, and as we then acknowledged them to be, a distinct and separate community, governed by their own peculiar laws and customs? We can never deny these principles, while fair dealing retains any hold of our conduct. Further, sir, it appears from this treaty, that the Indians who preferred to remain east of the river, expressed "to the President an anxious desire to engage in the pursuits of agriculture and civilized life in the country they then occupied," and we engaged to encourage those laudable purposes. Indeed, such pursuits had been recommended to the tribes, and patronized by the United States, for many years before this convention. Mr. Jefferson, in his message to Congress, as early as 1805, and when on the subject of our Indian relations, with his usual enlarged views of public policy, observes: "The aboriginal inhabitants of [this country], I have regarded with the commiseration their history inspires. Endowed with the faculties and the rights of men, breathing an ardent love of liberty and independence, and occupying a country which left them no desire but to be undisturbed, the stream of overflowing population from other regions directed itself on these shores. Without power to divert, or habits to contend against it, they have been overwhelmed by the current, or driven before it. Now, reduced within limits too narrow for the hunter state, humanity enjoins us to teach them agriculture and the domestic arts; to encourage them to that industry, which alone can enable them to maintain their place in existence; and to prepare them in time for that society, which, to bodily comforts, adds the improvement of the mind and morals. We have, therefore, liberally furnished them with the implements of husbandry and household use; we have placed among them instructors in the arts of first necessity; and they are covered with the aegis of the law against aggressors from among ourselves."[2] These, sir, are sentiments worthy of an illustrious statesman. None can fail to perceive the spirit of justice and humanity which Mr. Jefferson cherished

towards our Indian allies. He was, through his whole life, the firm unshrinking advocate of their rights, a patron of all their plans for moral improvement and elevation.

It will not be necessary to pursue the details of our treaty negotiations further. I beg leave to state, before I leave them, however, that with all the southwestern tribes of Indians we have similar treaties, not only the Cherokees, but the Creeks, Choctaws and Chickasaws, in the neighborhood of Georgia, Tennessee, Alabama, and Mississippi, hold our faith, repeatedly pledged to them, that we would respect their boundaries, repel aggressions, and protect and nourish them as our neighbors and friends; and to all these public and sacred compacts Georgia was a constant party. They were required, by an article [of the Constitution], to be submitted to the Senate of the United States for their advice and consent. They were so submitted; and Georgia, by her able Representatives in the Senate, united in the ratification of these same treaties, without, in any single instance, raising an exception, or interposing a constitutional difficulty or scruple.

Other branches of our political history shed abundant light upon this momentous question. When the Congress of the United States directed their cares to the future settlement and government of the vast and noble domains to the northwest of the river Ohio, ceded by the State of Virginia, among other matters which were deemed to be vitally connected with welfare of that region, was the condition and preservation of the Indian nations. The third article of the celebrated ordinance, for the government of the Northwestern Territory, is in the following words:

[2] Frelinghuysen's reference is to the Second Inaugural Address. See J. D. Richardson, ed., *Messages and Papers of the Presidents*, I, 380. [ED.'s NOTE]

Religion, morality, and knowledge, being necessary to good government and the happiness of mankind, schools and the means of education shall forever be encouraged. The utmost good faith shall always be observed towards the Indians; their lands and property shall never be taken from them without their consent; and, in their property, rights, and liberty, they never shall be invaded or disturbed, unless in just and lawful wars, authorized by Congress; but laws founded in justice and humanity shall, from time to time, be made, for preventing wrongs being done to them, and for preserving peace and friendship with them.

Sir, the more minutely we look into the proceedings of the Congress of 1787, the more deeply shall we venerate the wisdom and virtue, the largeness of views, and the political forecast, that blessed and illustrated the councils of our country. This solitary article would forever stand out, and alone sustain their reputation. . . .

How can Georgia, after all this, desire or attempt, and how can we quietly permit her, "to invade and disturb the property, rights, and liberty of the Indians"? And this, not only not "in just and lawful wars authorized by Congress," but in the time of profound peace, while the Cherokee lives in tranquil prosperity by her side. I press the inquiry—How can we tamely suffer these States to make laws, not only not "founded in justice and humanity," "for preventing wrongs being done to the Indians," but for the avowed purpose of inflicting the gross and wanton injustice of breaking up their Government —of abrogating their long-cherished customs, and of annihilating their existence as a distinct people?

The Congress of the United States, in [1790], in an act to regulate trade and intercourse with the Indian tribes; and again, by a similar act in 1802, still in force, distinctly recognised every material stipulation contained in the numerous treaties with the Indians. In fact, sir, these acts of legislation were passed expressly to effectuate our treaty stipulations.

These statutes refer to "the boundaries, as established by treaties between the United States and the various Indian tribes"; they next direct such "lines to be clearly ascertained, and distinctly marked" prohibit any citizen of the United States from crossing these lines, to hunt or settle, and authorize the employment of the public and military force of the Government, to prevent intrusion, and to expel trespassers upon Indian lands. The twelfth section of this important law most wisely guards the great object of Indian title from all public and private imposition, by enacting "that no purchase, grant, lease, or other conveyance of lands, or of any title or claim thereto, from any Indian or nation, or tribe of Indians, within the bounds of the United States, shall be of any validity in law or equity, unless the same be made by treaty or convention, entered into pursuant to the constitution."

I trust, sir, that this brief exposition of our policy, in relation to Indian affairs, establishes, beyond all controversy, the obligation of the United States to protect these tribes in the exercise and enjoyment of their civil and political rights. Sir, the question has ceased to be—What are our duties? An inquiry much more embarrassing is forced upon us: How shall we most plausibly, and with the least possible violence, break our faith? Sir, we repel the inquiry— we reject such an issue—and point the guardians of our public honor to the broad, plain [path] of faithful performance . . .

Wilson Lumpkin:

SPEECH BEFORE CONGRESS
(MAY 17, 1830)

Wilson Lumpkin remarks on the first page of his autobiography that his childhood on the Georgia frontier had been menaced by "frequent depredations from hostile and savage Indian neighbors. . . ."[1] Childhood memories were reinforced when, from 1818 to 1821, he worked, as a United States Commissioner, among the Creek and Cherokee Indians. Lumpkin became increasingly determined to see the final removal of the Indians from the State of Georgia. As a member of John Clarke's faction of the Democratic Party, the faction of the backwoodsmen opposed to George Troup's plantation-owner faction, Lumpkin was an early and an ardent supporter of Andrew Jackson. Re-elected to Congress in the year of Jackson's rise to power, Lumpkin knew that the opportune moment had arrived, and he determined to make the most of it. As noted above, he played a major role in pushing the removal bill through committee and in defending this controversial bill on the floor of the House of Representatives.

AMONGST my earliest recollections are the walls of an old fort, which gave protection to the women and children from the tomahawk and scalping knife of the Indians. And let me inform you, that, while the Indians have receded thousands of miles before the civilized population, in other sections of the Union, the frontier of Georgia has comparatively remained stationary. My present residence is not more than one day's travel from the place of the old fort to which I alluded. It is but part of a day's travel from my residence to the line of the Cherokee country.

In entering upon this branch of my subject, I find it necessary to summon up all the powers of philosophy, to restrain feelings of indignation and contempt for those who are at this time straining every nerve and using every effort to perpetuate on the people whom I represent the evils which they have borne for so many years; and whatever has, or may be said to the contrary, I do verily believe that no other State of this Union would have submitted, with equal patriotism, to the many ills and wrongs which we have received at the

[1] Wilson Lumpkin, *The Removal of the Cherokee Indians from Georgia* (New York: Dodd, Mead & Co., 1907), I, 1.

From Gales & Seaton's *Register of Debates in Congress*, VI, Part 2, 1020–1023.

hands of those who were bound by the strongest human obligations to aid in relieving us from Indian perplexities, give us justice, and assist in the advancement of our peace, happiness, and prosperity.

Georgia, sir, is one of the good old thirteen States; she entered the Union upon an equal footing with any of her sisters. She claims no superiority, but contends for equality. That sovereignty which she concedes to all the rest, and would at any time unite with them in defending from all encroachment, she will maintain for herself. Our social compact, upon which we stand as a State, gives you the metes and bounds of our sovereignty; and within the limits therein defined and pointed out, our State authorities claim entire and complete jurisdiction over soil and population, regardless of complexion.

The boundaries of Georgia have been defined, recognized, and admitted, by circumstances of a peculiar kind. Her litigations in relation to boundary and title to her soil may justly be considered as having been settled "according to law." Her boundaries are not only admitted by her sister States, but by this General Government; and every individual who administered any part of it, executive or legislative, must recollect that the faith of this Government has stood pledged for twenty-eight years past, to relieve Georgia from the embarrassment of Indian population. It is known to every member of this Congress, that this pledge was no gratuity to Georgia. No, sir, it was for and in consideration of the two entire States of Alabama and Mississippi.

I feel disposed to pity those who make the weak and false plea of inability, founded on the words "reasonable and peaceable," whenever I hear it made.

Such pettifogging quibbles deserve the contempt of a statesman. No man is fit to be a Congressman, who does not know that the General Government might, many years ago, upon both reasonable and peaceable terms, have removed every Indian from Georgia.

But, sir, upon this subject, this Government has been wanting in good faith to Georgia. It has, by its own acts and policy, forced the Indians to remain in Georgia, by the purchase of their lands in the adjoining States, and by holding out to the Indians strong inducements to remain where they are; by the expenditure of vast sums of money, spent in changing the habits of the savage for those of civilized life. All this was in itself right and proper; it has my hearty approbation; but it should not have been done at the expense of Georgia. The Government, long after it was bound to extinguish the title of the Indians to all the lands in Georgia, has actually forced the Cherokees from their lands in other States, settled them upon Georgia lands, and aided in furnishing the means to create the Cherokee aristocracy.

Sir, I blame not the Indians; I commiserate their case. I have considerable acquaintance with the Cherokees, and amongst them I have seen much to admire. To me, they are in many respects an interesting people. If the wicked influence of designing men, veiled in the garb of philanthropy and christian benevolence, should excite the Cherokees to a course that will end in their speedy destruction, I now call upon this Congress, and the whole American people, not to charge the Georgians with this sin; but let it be remembered that it is the fruit of cant and fanaticism, emanating from the land of steady habits, from the boasted progeny of the pilgrims and puritans.

Sir, my State stands charged before this House, before the nation, and before the whole world, with cruelty and oppression towards the Indians. I deny the charge, and demand proof from those who made it.

I have labored, as one of your committee, day and night, in examining every thing which has any connexion with the history of this subject. Amongst other duties, we have examined all the various laws of the colonial and State Governments in relation to the Indians. The selection made and submitted, has long since been in the hands of every gentleman of this House. Let the laws of other States be compared with those which are the subject of complaint, and it must then be admitted by every candid man that the States complained of stand pre-eminent in humanity, mildness, and generosity towards the Indians.

Georgia, it is true, has slaves; but she did not make them such; she found them upon her hands when she became a sovereign State. She never has, by her legislation, changed the state of freedom to slavery. If she has ever owned an Indian slave, it has never come to my knowledge; but more than one of the other States of this Union have not only reduced Indians to a state of slavery, but have treated them as brutes, destitute of any human rights—depriving them of their own modes of worshipping Deity—hunting them as wild beasts for slaughter—holding out rewards for their scalps, and even giving premiums for the raising of a certain breed of dogs, called bloodhounds, to hunt savages, that they might procure their scalps, and obtain the reward

offered by Government for them. Sir, compare this legislation with that of Georgia, and let the guilty be put to shame.

Should I be censured for going to the history of past times—a century or two back; should I be accused of visiting the sins of the fathers on the children, permit me to say, I hold in my hand a pamphlet, recently published in Boston, and said to have been written by the chief secretary of the new sect, who is also said to be the author of "William Penn";[2] and those who will read this pamphlet, written at the present day, will perceive a more savage, superstitious, and diabolical spirit, than was ever possessed by the authors of the pow-wow, scalping, slave, and dog laws. I will give you a few extracts from this pamphlet, which purports to be an article copied from the *American Monthly Magazine,* page 14.

"The Indians had better stand to their arms and be exterminated than march farther onwards to the Pacific, in the faith that the coming tide of civilized population will not sweep them forever until they mingle in its depths. Better thus than remain to be trampled as the serfs of Georgia, to have their faces ground by the pride and oppressions of their slave-holding neighbors, to be exterminated by the more powerful, and not less sure, though slower operation of the vices of the whites." "God forbid that the prayers which have ascended for the Indians, and the exertions which may be made in their behalf, should fail; it would be better that half the states in the Union were annihilated,

2 "William Penn" was Jeremiah Evarts, secretary of the American Board of Foreign Missions, whose twenty-four letters appeared in *The National Intelligencer.* This quotation is not found in these letters. [ED.'s NOTE]

and the remnant left powerful in holiness, strong in the prevalence of virtue, than that the whole nation should be stained with guilt, and sooner or later disorganized by the self-destroying energies of wickedness. We would rather have a civil war, were there no other alternative, than avoid it by taking shelter in crime; for besides that, in our faith, it would be better for the universe to be annihilated, than for one jot or tittle of the law of God to be broken, we know that such a shelter would only prove the prison house of vengeance and despair. We would take up arms for the Indians, in such a war, with as much confidence of our duty, as we would stand with our bayonets on the shores of the Atlantic, to repel the assaults of the most barbarous invader. Perhaps we do wrong to make even the supposition: for it can never come to this. But, let any thing come upon us, rather than the stain and curse of such perfidy as has been contemplated. Let the vials of God's wrath be poured out in plague, and storm, and desolation; let our navies be scattered to the four winds of heaven; let our corn be blasted in the fields; let our first born be consumed with the stroke of the pestilence; let us be visited with earthquakes, and given as a prey to the devouring fire; but let us not be left to commit so great an outrage on the law of nations and of God; let us not be abandoned to the degradation of national perjury, and, as its certain consequence, to some signal addition of national wo[e]. Let us listen to the warning voice which comes to us from the destruction of Israel."

The pamphlet from which I have read contains 72 pages, and is interspersed throughout with a spirit corresponding with what I have read. Sir, shall I express my surprise at this "christian party in politics," who condemn all their brethren who will not unite with them in all their machinery of societies and schemes for governing public opinion in this land of freedom? or shall I remember that if the wicked one himself can assume the form of an angel of light to deceive and effect his diabolical purposes, then we need not be surprised to see the children walking in the footsteps of their parents? The fallacious matter contained in this pamphlet, and its senior brother, "William Penn," we shall find to be strong ground relied upon here. Our opponents here will be found in close union with these concert brethren. And here it is, sir, for the first time, we find any thing like a tangible form in the opposition to Indian emigration, sustained and encouraged as it has been by every administration, from President Jefferson to Mr. Adams, inclusive; we have never before seen a concerted and united opposition, nor has any individual, who had any pretensions to the first honors of the country, heretofore ventured to oppose this system.

In the course of the last year, the numbers over the signature of "William Penn" appeared in the *National Intelligencer*, and, although said to be written by a very pious man, deeply merged in missionary efforts, they evidently have much more of the character of the politician and lawyer than that of an humble missionary. At the proper moment for effect, too, we see the distinguished orator of the West, he who once filled the chair which you now occupy, entering upon this subject with his usual zeal and ingenuity. This Indian subject was introduced into one of his set speeches, professedly on the subject of African colonization. But the two subjects are adroitly blended together, and were designed as a cutting philippic upon President Jackson and his administration, and, at the same time, admirably calculated to organize his political co-workers in every part of the Union. I was not surprised at his expressions of deep feelings of interest for the suffering sons of Africa and the forest. It was to be expected from a popular speech-maker. But I confess the pious part of his address shocked my better feelings. If I had been ignorant of the gentleman's character I should really have considered him a preacher of righteousness, deeply imbued with the spirit of the age!

Where do you find one solitary opponent of President Jackson in favor of the measure on your table? I do not know one. Sir, I have tried to prevent party considerations from operating on this question; but our opponents are an organized band; they go in a solid column. The friends of the administration are by no means united upon many subjects of general policy; each one thinks and acts for himself; but shall our differences upon other subjects operate upon our judgments in making up an opinion upon this important subject? Your attention has been called to it in the forcible language of truth, by your venerable Chief Magistrate. It is sustained by reason, experience, humanity, and every consideration of wise policy. It is a measure of great importance to the interest, peace, and harmony of many of the states; and to the poor afflicted and perishing Indians, it is a measure of salvation. No man living entertains kinder feelings to the Indians than Andrew Jackson. If any President of the United States has deserved the appellation of friend and father to the Indians, it is him who is now at the helm. Having been the instrument of the Government to chastise them in times that are gone by, so far as to bring them to a knowledge of their true condition and duty, he is the better qualified to sympathize with them in all their afflictions. He not only is, but has long been, their true friend and benefactor. This opposition is not to the policy proposed, but to the man who recommends it. I, therefore, trust his friends will not be found in the ranks of the enemy. I trust in God, more are they who are for us, than those who are against us. The opposition reminds me of Jonah's gourd, which sprung up in a night and perished in a day. It could bear the light and heat of but a single day, because there was a canker at the root. The present opposition cannot stand before the light of truth, reason, and sound policy—it will soon pass away.

Upon this question, our political opponents have availed themselves of the aid of enthusiastic religionists, to pull down the administration of President Jackson. Sir, pure religion will aid and strengthen any cause; but the undefiled religion of the Cross is a separate and distinct thing, in its nature and principles, from the noisy cant of these pretenders, who have cost this Government, since the commencement of the present session of Congress, considerably upwards of $100,000 by their various intermeddlings with the political concerns of the country. Who compose this "christian party in politics," here and elsewhere? Are they those individuals who are most distinguished for morality and virtue? I will leave these questions to be answered by others, and pass on to some further notice of the Boston pamphlet, from which we shall, no doubt, have many quotations before we get through this discussion.

It is the statements found in these pamphlets and magazines, which are relied on as truth, that have induced so many worthy people at a distance to espouse the cause of Indian sovereignty, as assumed by the Cherokees. The general condition of the Cherokees, in these publications, is represented as being quite as comfortable and prosperous— yes, sir, and as enlightened, too, as the white population in most of the states. Compare the pictures drawn by these pamphlet writers and memorialists of the concert school, in which they have painted Georgia on the one side, and the Cherokee sovereignty on the other. From these publications, not only the stranger in a foreign land but the honest laboring people of New England, who stay at home, and would mind their own business if let alone by these canting fanatics, verily believe that the Georgians are the worst of all savages; that they can neither read nor write; that they are infidels, deists, and atheists; and they never hear a gospel sermon, except from a New England missionary. Upon the other hand, they are taught to believe that the Cherokee Indians are the most prosperous, enlightened, and religious nation of people on earth—except, indeed, the nation of New England. These Boston writers are not a people who work for nothing and find themselves. No, sir, I entertain no doubt but that they are well paid for all "their labors of love" in the cause of Cherokee sovereignty.

The Cherokees receive large annuities from this Government; they have a rich treasury, and their Northern allies understand giving a saving direction to their financial disbursements. These Northern intruders are numerous and

influential among the Cherokees. One religious Board to the North (of whom "William Penn" is chief secretary) furnishes the southern tribes of Indians with upwards of twenty stationary missionaries, besides superintendents, mechanics, &c., &c., chiefly composed of our northern friends. No doubt, sir, but President Ross himself, with all his official subordinates, has long since found it expedient to yield the chief control of the purse and the press (which you know are said to be the strength of nations) to his more skilful and eagle-eyed friends and allies. But for these annuities, we should not have been encumbered, throughout the session, with memorials from Maine to Steubenville, in Ohio. These self-interested reporters of the state and condition of the Cherokee Indians tell you they are already a civilized and christianized people.

Abounding in the necessary comforts of domestic and agricultural life, their civil, political, and religious advancement is ostentatiously compared with the whites in some of the States; and, for proof of their statements, they refer you to their hireling letter writers, and their magazines and newspapers; and the statements drawn from these sources are relied on by a certain portion of the community, in and out of this House, in preference to any testimony, whatever may be the merit of the source from which it emanates. Now, sir, I will tell you how far these statements are to be relied upon. I have carefully and repeatedly examined all these magazine and pamphlet publications. They contain a great deal of truth, but not the whole truth, and nothing else but the truth. These publications remind me of a long exploring tour which I made to the West, near twenty years ago. On my return home, my friends and neighbors called in, to hear the news from the western country. I described to them the rich and fertile lands of the Mississippi, its bountiful productions, &c.; and before I had got through with the good things, they said, "it is enough, let us all remove to the good country."

But when I told them of the evil things, and gave them the whole truth, they changed their hasty opinions, and concluded it would be best to remain in their beloved Georgia. Sir, the application of this story is easy—every gentleman can make it for himself. But I promised to inform you how far these magazine statements were entitled to credit; but, before I begin, I will refer you to my list of witnesses. They may be found amongst the Senators and Representatives of the present Congress, from the states bordering on the Cherokee country. I could multiply testimony to bear me out in all that I have or shall say on this subject; but, in law, we consider every word established by the corroborating testimony of two or three witnesses. I admit we do find in the Cherokee country many families enjoying all the common comforts of civil and domestic life, and possessing the necessary means to secure these enjoyments. Moreover, we find a number of schools and houses built for religious worship. Many of these comfortable families, too, are composed of natives born in the Cherokee country. But the principal part of these enjoyments are confined to the blood of the white man, either in whole or in part. But few, very few of the real Indians participate largely in these blessings. A large portion of the full blooded Cherokees still remain a poor degraded race of human beings. As to the proportion that are comfortable, or otherwise, I cannot speak from my own personal knowledge with any degree of certainty; but, from what I have seen, I can readily conclude that but a very small portion of the real Indians are in a state of improvement, whilst their lords and rulers are white men, and the descendants of white men, enjoying the fat of the land, and enjoying exclusively the Government annuities, upon which they foster, feed, and clothe the most violent and dangerous enemies of our civil institutions.

While the smallest intrusion (as it is called) by the frontier citizens of Georgia on the lands occupied by the Cherokees, excites the fiery indignation of the fanatics, from one end of the chain of concert and coalition to the other, do we not find an annual increase of intruders, from these philanthropic ranks, flocking in upon the poor Cherokees, like the caterpillars and locusts of Egypt, leaving a barren waste behind them? Yes, sir, these are the intruders who devour the substance which of right belongs to the poor perishing part of the Cherokees. They divide the spoil with the Cherokee rulers, and leave the common Indians to struggle with want and misery, without hope of bettering their condition by any change but that of joining their brethren west of the Mississippi.

The inhumanity of Georgia, so much complained of, is nothing more nor less than the extension of her laws and jurisdiction over this mingled and misguided population who are found within her acknowledged limits.

And what, I would ask, is to be found in all this, that is so very alarming? Sir, I have endeavored to tear the mask from this subject, that the character and complexion of this opposition might be seen and known. The absolute rulers of the Cherokee country, like other men, love office, distinction, and power. They are enjoying great and peculiar benefits. They do not like the idea of becoming private citizens. It is with great reluctance they yield up their stewardship. They know they have not been faithful to the interest of the poor degraded Indians. They know the great mass of their people have been left to suffer in want and ignorance, whilst they have spent their substance in forming foreign alliances with an enthusiastic, selfish, and money-loving people. These men, when incorporated into the political family of Georgia, cannot calculate on becoming at once the Randolphs of the State. And if they join the western Cherokees, they cannot carry with them their present assumed sovereignty and rule. They will there find equals in many of their pioneer brethren. The Cadmus of the Cherokees, George Guess, and many others, are already there.[3] Yes, sir, these western Cherokees are in the full enjoyment of all the

blessings of their emigrating enterprise, and there is but one opinion among them as to their relative comfort and prospect of future blessings. All the various emigrants to the West so far agree as to authorize the assurance that no inducement could be offered to them strong enough to bring them back again.

The Cherokees and Creeks are charmed with their country, and to the many things which attach to their comfort in it. The New England farmers who have emigrated to the fertile valleys of the West, would as soon consent to return to the barren sand and sterile rocks of their native land, as a western Cherokee or Creek would return to the sepulchre of his forefathers.

Pages may be filled with a sublimated cant of the day, and in wailing over the departure of the Cherokees from the bones of their forefathers. But if the heads of these pretended mourners were waters, and their eyes were a fountain of tears, and they were to spend days and years in weeping over the departure of the Cherokees from Georgia, yet they will go. The tide of emigration, with the Indians as well as the whites, directs its course westwardly. . . .

[3] George Guess, better known as Sequoyah, devised the Cherokee alphabet and can be likened to Cadmus, mythical founder of Thebes. [ED's NOTE]

David Crockett:

FROM SPEECH BEFORE CONGRESS (MAY 19, 1830)

Born in Hawkins County, Tennessee, Davy Crockett lived wildly and became, at one time, a legendary teller of tall tales and a three-time member of the House of Representatives. He was (and is) a symbol of the American frontiersman and was, concurrently, a determined opponent, political and personal, of Andrew Jackson. It is not surprising that he opposed Jackson on this issue as on others. Like the Indians whom he failed to save, Davy Crockett became disheartened by Jackson's repeated victories. In 1836 he left for Texas and martyrdom at the Alamo.

MR. Crockett said, that, considering his very humble abilities, it might be expected that he should content himself with a silent vote; but, situated as he was, in relation to his colleagues, he felt it to be a duty to himself to explain the motives which governed him in the vote he should give on this bill. Gentlemen had already discussed the treaty-making power; and had done it much more ably than he could pretend to do. He should not therefore enter on that subject, but would merely make an explanation as to the reasons of his vote. He did not know whether a man (that is, a member of Congress) within 500 miles of his residence would give a similar vote; but he knew, at the same time, that he should give that vote with a clear conscience. He had his constituents to settle with, he was aware; and should like to please them as well as other gentlemen; but he had also a settlement to make at the bar of his God; and what his conscience dictated to be just and right he would do, be the consequences what they might. He believed that the people who had been kind enough to give him their suffrages, supposed him to be an honest man, or they would not have chosen him. If so, they could not but expect that he should act in the way he thought honest and right. He had always viewed the native Indian tribes of this country as a sovereign people. He believed they had been recognised as such from the very foundation of this government, and the United States were bound by treaty to protect them; it was their duty to do so. And as to giving the money of the

From *Speeches on the Passage of the Bill for the Removal of the Indians* (Boston: Perkins & Marvin, 1830), pp. 251–253.

American people for the purpose of removing them in the manner proposed, he would not do it. He would do that only for which he could answer to his God. Whether he could answer it before the people was comparatively nothing, though it was a great satisfaction to him to have the approbation of his constituents.

Mr. C. said he had served for seven years in a legislative body. But from the first hour he had entered a legislative hall, he had never known what party was in legislation; and God forbid he ever should. He went for the good of the country, and for that only. What he did as a legislator, he did conscientiously. He should love to go with his colleagues, and with the West and the South generally, if he could; but he never would let party govern him in a question of this great consequence.

He had many objections to the bill—some of them of a very serious character. One was, that he did not like to put half a million of money into the hands of the Executive, to be used in a manner which nobody could foresee, and which Congress was not to control. Another objection was, he did not wish to depart from the rule which had been observed towards the Indian nations from the foundation of the government. He considered the present application as the last alternative for these poor remnants of a once powerful people. Their only chance of aid was at the hands of Congress. Should its members turn a deaf ear to their cries, misery must be their fate. That was his candid opinion.

Mr. C. said he was often forcibly reminded of the remark made by the famous *Red Jacket,* in the rotunda of this building, when he was shown the panel which represented in sculpture the first landing of the Pilgrims, with an Indian chief presenting to them an ear of corn, in token of friendly welcome. The aged Indian said "that was good." The Indian said, he knew that they came from the Great Spirit, and he was willing to share the soil with his brothers from over the great water. But when he turned round to another panel representing Penn's treaty, he said "Ah! all's gone now." There was a great deal of truth in this short saying; and the present bill was a strong commentary upon it.

Mr. C. said that four counties of his district bordered on the Chickasaw country. He knew many of their tribe; and nothing should ever induce him to vote to drive them west of the Mississippi. He did not know what sort of a country it was in which they were to be settled. He would willingly appropriate money in order to send proper persons to examine the country. And when this had been done, and a fair and free treaty had been made with the tribes, if they were desirous of removing, he would vote an appropriation of any sum necessary; but till this had been done, he would not vote one cent. He could not clearly understand the extent of this bill. It seemed to go to the removal of all the Indians, in any State east of the Mississippi river, in which the United States owned any land. Now, there was a considerable number of them still neglected; there was a considerable number of them in Tennessee, and the United States government owned no land in that State, north and east of the congressional reservation line. No man could be more willing to see them remove than he was, if it could be done in a manner agreeable to themselves; but not otherwise. He knew personally that a part of the tribe of the Cherokees were unwilling to go. When the proposal was made to them, they said, "No: we will take death here at our homes. Let them come and tomahawk us here at home: we are willing to die, but never to remove." He had heard them use this language. Many different constructions might be put upon this bill. One of the first things which had set him against the bill, was the letter from the secretary of war to colonel Montgomery—from which it appeared that the Indians had been intruded upon. Orders had been issued to turn them all off except the heads of the Indian families, or such as possessed improvements. Government had taken measures to purchase land from the Indians who had gone to Arkansas. If this bill should pass, the same plan would be carried further; they would send and buy them out, and put white men upon their land. It had never been known that white men and Indians could live together; and in this case, the Indians were to have no privileges allowed them, while the white men were to have all. Now, if this was not oppression with a vengeance, he did not know what was. It was the language of the bill, and of its friends, that the Indians were not to be driven off against their will. He knew the Indians were unwilling to go: and therefore he could not consent to place them in a situation where they would be obliged to go. He could not stand that. He knew that he stood alone, having, perhaps, none of his colleagues from his state agreeing in sentiment. He could not help that. He knew that he should return to his home glad and light in heart, if he voted against the bill. He felt that it was his wish and purpose to serve his constituents honestly, according to the light of his conscience. The moment he should exchange his conscience for mere party views, he hoped his Maker would no longer suffer him to exist. He spoke the truth in saying so. If he should be the only member of that House who voted against the bill, and the only man in the United States who disapproved it, he would still vote against it; and it would be matter of rejoicing to him till the day he died, that he had given the vote. He had been told that he should be prostrated; but if so, he would have the consolation of conscience. He would obey that power, and gloried in the deed. He cared not for popularity, unless it could be obtained by upright means. He had seen much to disgust him here; and he did not wish to represent his fellow-citizens, unless he could be permitted to act conscientiously. He had been told that he did not understand English grammar. That was very true. He had never been six months at school in his life: he had raised himself by the labor of his hands. But he did not, on that account, yield up his privilege as the representative of freemen on this floor.[1] Humble as he was, he meant to exercise his privilege. He had been charged with not representing his constituents. If the fact was so, the error (said Mr. C.) is here (touching his head), not here (laying his hand upon his heart). He never had possessed wealth or education, but he had ever been animated by an independent spirit; and he trusted to prove it on the present occasion.

[1] Colonel Crockett represents more voters than any member of Congress, except Mr. Duncan of Illinois. The reason is, the great influx of population since the State was formed into districts. There were 20,000 voters in colonel Crockett's district more than a year ago. There are probably more than 22,000 now.

MEMORIAL OF THE CHEROKEE NATION (JULY 17, 1830)

Appeals such as Representative Crockett's were in vain. On the 26th of May, 1830, Lumpkin's bill passed the House by a vote of 102 to 97. The Senate concurred with the House's amendments, and the bill was signed into law on the 28th of May. The enactment did not revoke the treaties then in force between the United States and the Cherokee nation, and the Cherokees appealed to the American people and urged them not to break the treaties. "We wish," wrote the assembled leaders of the nation, "to remain on the land of our fathers."

SOME months ago a delegation was appointed by the constituted authorities of the Cherokee nation to repair to the city of Washington, and in behalf of this nation, to lay before the government of the United States such representations as should seem most likely to secure to us, as a people, that protection, aid, and good neighborhood, which had been so often promised to us, and of which we stand in great need. Soon after their arrival in the city they presented to congress a petition from our national council, asking for the interposition of that body in our behalf, especially with reference to the laws of Georgia; which were suspended in a most terrifying manner over a large part of our population, and protesting in the most decided terms against the operation of these laws. In the course of the winter they presented petitions to congress, signed by more than four thousand of our citizens, including probably more than nineteen-twentieths, and for aught we can tell, ninety-nine hundredths, of the adult males of the nation. . . , pleading with the assembled representatives of the American people, that the solemn engagements between their fathers and our fathers may be preserved, as they have been till recently, in full force and continued operation; asking, in a word, for protection against threatened usurpation and for a faithful execution for a guaranty which is perfectly plain in its meaning, has been repeatedly and rigidly endorsed in our favour, and has received the sanction of the government of the United States for nearly forty years.

More than a year ago we were officially given to understand by the secretary of war, that the president could not protect us against the laws of Georgia. This information was entirely unexpected; as it went upon the principle, that treaties made between the United States and the Cherokee nation have no power to withstand the legislation of separate states; and of course, that they have no efficacy whatever, but leave our people to the mercy of the neighboring whites, whose supposed interests would be promoted by our expulsion, or extermination. It would be impossible to describe the sorrow, which affected our minds on learning that the chief magistrate of the United States had come to this conclusion, that all his illustrious predecessors had held intercourse with us on principles which could not be sustained; that they had made promises of vital importance to us, which could not be fulfilled—promises made hundreds of times in almost every conceivable manner,—often in the form of solemn treaties, sometimes in letters written by the chief magistrate with his own hand, very often in letters written by the secretary of war under his direction, sometimes orally by the president and the secretary to our chiefs, and frequently and always, both orally and in writing by the agent of the United States residing among us, whose most important business it was, to see the guaranty of the United States faithfully executed.

Soon after the war of the revolution, as we have learned from our fathers, the Cherokees looked upon the promises of the whites with great distrust and suspicion; but the frank and magnanimous conduct of General Washington did much to allay these feelings. The perseverance of successive presidents, and especially of Mr. Jefferson, in the same course of policy, and in the constant assurance that our country should remain inviolate, except so far as we voluntarily ceded it, nearly banished anxiety in regard to encroachments from the whites. To this result the aid which we received from the United States in the attempts of our people to become civilized, and the kind efforts of benevo-

lent societies, have greatly contributed. Of late years, however, much solicitude was occasioned among our people by the claims of Georgia. This solicitude arose from the apprehension, that by extreme importunity, threats, and other undue influence, a treaty would be made, which should cede the territory, and thus compel the inhabitants to remove. But it never occurred to us for a moment, that without any new treaty, without any assent of our rulers and people, without even a pretended compact, and against our vehement and unanimous protestations, we should be delivered over to the discretion of those, who had declared by a legislative act, that they wanted the Cherokee lands and would have them.

Finding that relief could not be obtained from the chief magistrate, and not doubting that our claim to protection was just, we made our application to congress. During four long months our delegation waited, at the doors of the national legislature of the United States, and the people at home, in the most painful suspense, to learn in what manner our application would be answered; and, now that congress has adjourned, on the very day before the date fixed by Georgia for the extension of her oppressive laws over the greater part of our country, the distressing intelligence has been received that we have received no answer at all; and no department of the government has assured us, that we are to receive the desired protection. But just at the close of the session, an act was passed, by which an half a million of dollars was appropriated towards effecting a removal of Indians; and we have great reason to fear that the influence of this act will be brought to bear most injuriously upon us. The passage of this act was certainly understood by the representatives of Georgia as abandoning us to the oppressive and cruel measures of the state, and as sanctioning the opinion that treaties with Indians do not restrain state legislation. We are informed by those, who are competent to judge, that the recent act does not admit of such construction; but that the passage of it, under the actual circumstances of the controversy, will be considered as sanctioning the pretensions of Georgia, there is too much reason to fear.

Thus have we realized, with heavy hearts, that our supplication has not been heard; that the protection heretofore experienced is now to be withheld; that the guaranty, in consequence of which our fathers laid aside their arms and ceded the best portions of their country, means nothing; and that we must either emigrate to an unknown region and leave the pleasant land to which we have the strongest attachment, or submit to the legislation of a state, which has already made our people outlaws, and enacted that any Cherokee, who shall endeavor to prevent the selling of his country, shall be imprisoned in the penitentiary of Georgia not less than four years. To our countrymen this has been melancholy intelligence, and with the most bitter disappointment has it been received.

But in the midst of our sorrows, we do not forget our obligations to our friends and benefactors. It was with sensations of inexpressible joy that we have learned that the voice of thousands, in many parts of the United States, has been raised in our behalf, and numerous memorials offered in our favor, in both houses of congress. To those numerous friends, who have thus sympathized with us in our low estate, we tender our grateful acknowledgements. In pleading our cause, they have pleaded the cause of the poor and defenceless throughout the world. Our special thanks are due, however, to those honorable men, who so ably and eloquently asserted our rights, in both branches of the national legislature. Their efforts will be appreciated wherever the merits of this question shall be known; and we cannot but think, that they have secured for themselves a permanent reputation among the disinterested advocates of humanity, equal rights, justice, and good faith. We even cherish the hope, that these efforts, seconded and followed by others of a similar character, will yet be available, so far as to mitigate our sufferings, if not to effect our entire deliverance.

Before we close this address, permit us to state what we conceive to be our relations with the United States. After the peace of 1783, the Cherokees were an independent people; absolutely so, as much as any people on earth. They had been allies to Great Britain, and as a faithful ally took a part in the colonial war on her side. They had placed themselves under her protection, and had they, without cause, declared hostility against their protector, and had the colonies been subdued, what might not have been their fate? But her power on this continent was broken. She acknowledged the independence of the United States, and made peace. The Cherokees therefore stood alone; and, in these circumstances, continued the war. They were then under no obligations to the United States any more than to Great Britain, France or Spain. The United States never subjugated the Cherokees; on the contrary, our fathers remained in possession of their country, and with arms in their hands.

The people of the United States sought a peace; and, in 1785, the treaty of Hopewell was formed, by which the Cherokees came under the protection of the United States, and submitted to such limitations of sovereignty as are mentioned in that instrument. None of these limitations, however, affected, in the slightest degree, their rights of self-government and inviolate territory. The citizens of the United States had no right of passage through the Cherokee country till the year 1791, and then only in one direction, and by an express treaty stipulation. When the federal constitution was adopted, the treaty of Hopewell was confirmed, with all other treaties, as the supreme law of the land. In 1791, the treaty of Holston was made, by which the sovereignty of the Cherokees was qualified as follows: The Cherokees acknowledged themselves to be under the protection of the United States, and of no other sovereign.—They engaged that they would not hold any treaty with a foreign power, with any separate state of the union, or with individuals. They agreed that the United States should have the exclusive right of regulating their trade; that the citizens of the United States should have a right of way in one direction through the Cherokee country; and that if an Indian should do injury to a citizen of the United States he should be delivered up to be tried and punished. A cession of lands was also made to the United States. On the other hand, the United States paid a sum of money; offered protection; engaged to punish citizens of the United States who should do any injury to the Cherokees; abandoned white settlers on Cherokee lands to the discretion of the Cherokees; stipulated that white men should not hunt on these lands, nor even enter the country without a passport; and gave a solemn guaranty of all Cherokee lands not ceded. This treaty is the basis of all subsequent compacts; and in none of

them are the relations of the parties at all changed.

The Cherokees have always fulfilled their engagements. They have never reclaimed those portions of sovereignty which they surrendered by the treaties of Hopewell and Holston. These portions were surrendered for the purpose of obtaining the guaranty which was recommended to them as the great equivalent. Had they refused to comply with their engagements, there is no doubt the United States would have enforced a compliance. Is the duty of fulfilling engagements on the other side less binding than it would be, if the Cherokees had the power of enforcing their just claims?

The people of the United States will have the fairness to reflect, that all the treaties between them and the Cherokees were made, at the solicitation, and for the benefit, of the whites; that valuable considerations were given for every stipulation, on the part of the United States; that it is impossible to reinstate the parties in their former situation, that there are now hundreds of thousands of citizens of the United States residing upon lands ceded by the Cherokees in these very treaties; and that our people have trusted their country to the guaranty of the United States. If this guaranty fails them, in what can they trust, and where can they look for protection?

We are aware, that some persons suppose it will be for our advantage to remove beyond the Mississippi. We think otherwise. Our people universally think otherwise. Thinking that it would be fatal to their interests, they have almost to a man sent their memorial to congress, deprecating the necessity of a removal. This question was distinctly before their minds when they signed their memorial. Not an adult person can be found, who has not an opinion on the subject, and if the people were to understand distinctly, that they could be protected against the laws of the neighboring states, there is probably not an adult person in the nation, who would think it best to remove; though possibly a few might emigrate individually. There are doubtless many, who would flee to an unknown country, however beset with dangers, privations and sufferings, rather than be sentenced to spend six years in a Georgia prison for advising one of their neighbors not to betray his country. And there are others who could not think of living as outlaws in their native land, exposed to numberless vexations, and excluded from being parties or witnesses in a court of justice. It is incredible that Georgia should ever have enacted the oppressive laws to which reference is here made, unless she had supposed that something extremely terrific in its character was necessary in order to make the Cherokees willing to remove. We are not willing to remove; and if we could be brought to this extremity, it would be not by argument, not because our judgment was satisfied, not because our condition will be improved; but only because we cannot endure to be deprived of our national and individual rights and subjected to a process of intolerable oppression.

We wish to remain on the land of our fathers. We have a perfect and original right to remain without interruption or molestation. The treaties with us, and laws of the United States made in pursuance of treaties, guaranty our residence and our privileges, and secure us against intruders. Our only request is, that these treaties may be fulfilled, and these laws executed.

But if we are compelled to leave our country, we see nothing but ruin before us. The country west of the Arkansas territory is unknown to us. From what we can learn of it, we have no prepossessions in its favor. All the inviting parts of it, as we believe, are preoccupied by various Indian nations, to which it has been assigned. They would regard us as intruders, and look upon us with an evil eye. The far greater part of that region is, beyond all controversy, badly supplied with wood and water; and no Indian tribe can live as agriculturists without these articles. All our neighbors, in case of our removal, though crowded into our near vicinity, would speak a language totally different from ours, and practice different customs. The original possessors of that region are now wandering savages lurking for prey in the neighborhood. They have always been at war, and would be easily tempted to turn their arms against peaceful emigrants. Were the country to which we are urged much better than it is represented to be, and were it free from the objections which we have made to it, still it is not the land of our birth, nor of our affections. It contains neither the scenes of our childhood, nor the graves of our fathers.

The removal of families to a new country, even under the most favorable auspices, and when the spirits are sustained by pleasing visions of the future, is attended with much depression of mind and sinking of heart. This is the case, when the removal is a matter of decided preference, and when the persons concerned are in early youth or vigorous manhood. Judge, then, what must be the circumstances of a removal, when a whole community, embracing persons of all classes and every description, from the infant to the man of extreme old age, the sick, the blind, the lame, the improvident, the reckless, the desperate, as well as the prudent, the considerate, the industrious, are compelled to remove by odious and intolerable vexations and persecutions, brought upon them in the forms of law, when all will agree only in this, that they have been cruelly robbed of their country, in violation of the most solemn compacts, which it is possible for communities to form with each other; and that, if they should make themselves comfortable in their new residence, they have nothing to expect hereafter but to be the victims of a future legalized robbery!

Such we deem, and are absolutely certain, will be the feelings of the whole Cherokee people, if they are forcibly compelled, by the laws of Georgia, to remove; and with these feelings, how is it possible that we should pursue our present course of improvement, or avoid sinking into utter despondency? We have been called a poor, ignorant, and degraded people. We certainly are not rich; nor have we ever boasted of our knowledge, or our moral or intellectual elevation. But there is not a man within our limits so ignorant as not to know that he has a right to live on the land of his fathers, in the possession of his immemorial privileges, and that this right has been acknowleged and guaranteed by the United States; nor is there a man so degraded as not to feel a keen sense of injury, on being deprived of this right and driven into exile.

It is under a sense of the most pungent feelings that we make this, perhaps our last appeal to the good people of the United States. It cannot be that the community we are addressing, remarkable for its intelligence and religious sensibilities, and pre-eminent for its devotion to the rights of man, will lay aside this appeal, without considering that we stand in need of its sympathy and commiseration. We know that to the Christian and to the philanthropist the voice of our multiplied sorrows and fiery trials will not appear as an idle tale. In our own land, on our own soil, and in our own dwellings, which we reared for our wives and for our little ones, when there was peace on our mountains and in our valleys, we are encountering troubles which cannot but try our very souls. But shall we, on account of these troubles, forsake our beloved country? Shall we be compelled by a civilized and Christian people, with whom we have lived in perfect peace for the last forty years, and for whom we have willingly bled in war, to bid a final adieu to our homes, our farms, our streams and our beautiful forests? No. We are still firm. We intend still to cling, with our wonted affection, to the land which gave us birth, and which, every day of our lives, brings to us new and stronger ties of attachment. We appeal to the judge of all the earth, who will finally award us justice, and to the good sense of the American people, whether we are intruders upon the land of others. Our consciences bear us witness that we are the invaders of no man's rights—we have robbed no man of his territory—we have usurped no man's authority, nor have we deprived any one of his unalienable privileges. How then shall we indirectly confess the right of another people to our land by leaving it forever? On the soil which contains the ashes of our beloved men we wish to live—on this soil we wish to die.

We intreat those to whom the foregoing paragraphs are addressed, to remember the great law of love. "Do to others as ye would that others should do to you"—Let them remember that of all nations on the earth, they are under the greatest obligation to obey this law. We pray them to remember that, for the sake of principle, their forefathers were *compelled* to leave, therefore *driven* from the old world, and that the winds of persecution wafted them over the great waters and landed them on the shores of the new world, when the Indian was the sole lord and proprietor of these extensive domains—Let them remember in what way they were received by the savage of America, when power was in his hand, and his ferocity could not be restrained by any human arm. We urge them to bear in mind, that those who would now ask of them a cup of cold water, and a spot of earth, a portion of their own patrimonial possessions, on which to live and die in peace, are the descendants of those, whose origin, as inhabitants of North America, history and tradition are alike insufficient to reveal. Let them bring to remembrance all these facts, and they *cannot*, and we are sure, they *will* not fail to remember, and sympathize with us in these our trials and sufferings.

LEWIS ROSS, pres't committee.

James Daniel,	George Sanders,
Jos. Vann,	Daniel Griffin, jun.
David Vann,	James Hamilton,
Edward Gunter,	Alex. McDaniel,
Richard Taylor,	Thos. Foreman,
John Baldridge,	John Timson.
Samuel Ward,	

W. S. Coodey, clerk.

GOING SNAKE, speaker of the council.

James Bigbey,	J. R. Daniel,
Deer-in-the-water,	Slim Fellow,
Charles Reese,	Situake,
Sleeping Rabbit,	De-gah-le-lu-ge,
Chu-nu-gee,	Robbin,
Bark,	Tah-lah-doo,
Laugh-at-mush,	Nah-hoo-lah,
Chuleowah,	White Path,
Turtle,	Ne-gah-we,
Walking Stick,	Dah-ye-ske.
Moses Parris,	

John Ridge, clerk of the council.
New Echota, C.N. July 17, 1830.

Andrew Jackson:

INDIAN REMOVAL AND THE GENERAL GOOD

The memorial of the Cherokee nation did not sway President Jackson from his course. Resolutely, more explicitly than a year before, he outlined his determination to see the Indian tribes removed to the West. If anything, Jackson's second Annual Message (December 6, 1830) was less conciliatory than his first.

IT gives me pleasure to announce to Congress that the benevolent policy of the Government, steadily pursued for nearly thirty years, in relation to the removal of the Indians beyond the white settlements is approaching . . . a happy consummation. Two important tribes, [the Choctaws and the Chickasaws], have accepted the provision made for their removal at the last session of Congress, and it believed that their example will induce the remaining tribes also to seek the same obvious advantages.

The consequences of a speedy removal will be important to the United States, to individual States, and to the Indians themselves. The pecuniary advantages which it promises to the Government are the least of its recommendations. It puts an end to all possible danger of collision between the authorities of the General and State Governments on account of the Indians. It will place a dense and civilized population in large tracts of country now occupied by a few savage hunters. By opening the whole territory between Tennessee on the north and Louisiana on the south to the settlement of the whites it will incalculably strengthen the southwestern frontier and render the adjacent States strong enough to repel future invasions without remote aid. It will relieve the whole State of Mississippi and the western part of Alabama of Indian occupancy, and enable those States to advance rapidly in population, wealth, and power. It will separate the Indians from immediate contact with settlements of whites; free them from the power of the States; enable them to pursue happiness in their own way and under their own rude institutions; will retard the progress of decay, which is lessening their numbers, and perhaps cause them gradually, under the protection of the Government and through the influence of good counsels, to cast off their savage habits and become an interesting, civilized, and Christian community. These consequences,

From second Annual Message, J. D. Richardson, ed., *A Compilation of the Messages and Papers of the Presidents,* II, 519–523.

some of them so certain and the rest so probable, make the complete execution of the plan sanctioned by Congress at their last session an object of much solicitude.[1]

Toward the aborigines of the country no one can indulge a more friendly feeling than myself, or would go further in attempting to reclaim them from their wandering habits and make them a happy, prosperous people. I have endeavored to impress upon them my own solemn convictions of the duties and powers of the General Government in relation to the State authorities. For the justice of the laws passed by the States within the scope of their reserved powers they are not responsible to this Government. As individuals we may entertain and express our opinions of their acts, but as a Government we have as little right to control them as we have to prescribe laws for other nations.

With a full understanding of the subject, the Choctaw and the Chickasaw tribes have with great unanimity determined to avail themselves of the liberal offers presented by the act of Congress, and have agreed to remove beyond the Mississippi River. Treaties have been made with them, which in due season will be submitted for consideration. In negotiating these treaties they were made to understand their true condition, and they have preferred maintaining their independence in the Western forests to submitting to the laws of the States in which they now reside. These treaties, being probably the last which will ever be made with them, are characterized by great liberality on the part of the Government. They give the Indians a liberal sum in consideration of their removal, and comfortable subsist-

ence on their arrival at their new homes. If it be their real interest to maintain a separate existence, they will there be at liberty to do so without the inconveniences and vexations to which they would unavoidably have been subject in Alabama and Mississippi.

Humanity has often wept over the fate of the aborigines of this country, and philanthropy has been long busily employed in devising means to avert it, but its progress has never for a moment been arrested, and one by one have many powerful tribes disappeared from the earth. To follow to the tomb the last of his race and to tread on the graves of extinct nations excite melancholy reflections. But true philanthropy reconciles the mind to these vicissitudes as it does to the extinction of one generation to make room for another. In the monuments and fortresses of an unknown people, spread over the extensive regions of the West, we behold the memorials of a once powerful race, which was exterminated or has disappeared to make room for the existing savage tribes. Nor is there anything in this which, upon a comprehensive view of the general interests of the human race, is to be regretted. Philanthropy could not wish to see this continent restored to the condition in which it was found by our forefathers. What good man would prefer a country covered with forests and ranged by a few thousand savages to our extensive Republic, studded with cities, towns, and prosperous farms, embellished with all the improvements which art can devise or industry execute, occupied by more than 12,000,000 happy people, and filled with all the blessings of liberty, civilization, and religion?

The present policy of the Government is but a continuation of the same pro-

[1] A reference to Wilson Lumpkin's bill for Indian removal. [ED.'s NOTE]

gressive change by a milder process. The tribes which occupied the countries now constituting the Eastern States were annihilated or have melted away to make room for the whites. The waves of population and civilization are rolling to the westward, and we now propose to acquire the countries occupied by the red men of the South and West by a fair exchange, and, at the expense of the United States, to send them to a land where their existence may be prolonged and perhaps made perpetual. Doubtless it will be painful to leave the graves of their fathers; but what do they more than our ancestors did or than our children are now doing? To better their condition in an unknown land our forefathers left all that was dear in earthly objects. Our children by thousands yearly leave the land of their birth to seek new homes in distant regions. Does Humanity weep at these painful separations from everything, animate and inanimate, with which the young heart has become entwined? Far from it. It is rather a source of joy that our country affords scope where our young population may range unconstrained in body or in mind, developing the power and faculties of man in their highest perfection. These remove hundreds and almost thousands of miles at their own expense, purchase the lands they occupy, and support themselves at their new homes from the moment of their arrival. Can it be cruel in this Government when, by events which it can not control, the Indian is made discontented in his ancient home to purchase his lands, to give him a new and extensive territory, to pay the expense of his removal, and support him a year in his new abode? How many thousands of our own people would gladly embrace the opportunity of removing to the West on such condi-

tions! If the offers made to the Indians were extended to them, they would be hailed with gratitude and joy.

And is it supposed that the wandering savage has a stronger attachment to his home than the settled, civilized Christian? Is it more afflicting to him to leave the graves of his fathers than it is to our brothers and children? Rightly considered, the policy of the General Government toward the red man is not only liberal, but generous. He is unwilling to submit to the laws of the States and mingle with their population. To save him from this alternative, or perhaps utter annihilation, the General Government kindly offers him a new home, and proposes to pay the whole expense of his removal and settlement.

In the consummation of a policy originating at an early period, and steadily pursued by every Administration within the present century—so just to the States and so generous to the Indians—the Executive feels it has a right to expect the cooperation of Congress and of all good and disinterested men. The States, moveover, have a right to demand it. It was substantially a part of the compact which made them members of our Confederacy. With Georgia there is an express contract; with the new States an implied one of equal obligation. Why, in authorizing Ohio, Indiana, Illinois, Missouri, Mississippi, and Alabama to form constitutions and become separate States, did Congress include within their limits extensive tracts of Indian lands, and, in some instances, powerful Indian tribes? Was it not understood by both parties that the power of the States was to be coextensive with their limits, and that with all convenient dispatch the General Government should extinguish the Indian title and remove every obstruction to the complete jurisdiction of the State governments over the soil? Probably not one of those States would have accepted a separate existence—certainly it would never have been granted by Congress—had it been understood that they were to be confined forever to those small portions of their nominal territory the Indian title to which had at the time been extinguished.

It is, therefore, a duty which this Government owes to the new States to extinguish as soon as possible the Indian title to all lands which Congress themselves have included within their limits. When this is done the duties of the General Government in relation to the States and the Indians within their limits are at an end. The Indians may leave the State or not, as they choose. The purchase of their lands does not alter in the least their personal relations with the State government. No act of the General Government has ever been deemed necessary to give the States jurisdiction over the persons of the Indians. That they possess by virtue of their sovereign power within their own limits in as full a manner before as after the purchase of the Indian lands; nor can this Government add to or diminish it.

May we not hope, therefore, that all good citizens, and none more zealously than those who think the Indians oppressed by subjection to the laws of the States, will unite in attempting to open the eyes of those children of the forest to their true condition, and by a speedy removal to relieve them from all the evils, real or imaginary, present or prospective, with which they may be supposed to be threatened.

RESOLUTION AND STATEMENTS
OF THE MISSIONARIES

Although the appeals of the Cherokees had thus far been in vain, the missionaries then working among the tribe decided to brave the wrath of the State of Georgia. They gathered at New Echota, the Cherokee capital, and made public (December 29, 1830) their view of the controversy.

AT a meeting held at New Echota, December 29th, 1830, the following persons were present:

Rev. Daniel S. Butrick, Rev. Wm. Chamberlin, Rev. Wm. Potter, Rev. S. A. Worcester, Rev. John Thompson, Missionaries of the American Board of Commissioners for Foreign Missions.

Mr. Isaac Proctor, Doct. Elizur Butler, Mr. John C. Elsworth, Mr. Wm. Holland, Assistant missionaries of the A.B.C.F.M.

Rev. Gottlieb Byhan, Rev. H. G. Clauder, Missionaries of the U. Brethren's Church.

Rev. Evan Jones, Missionary of the American Baptist Board of Foreign Missions

Daniel S. Butrick was chosen chairman of the meeting, and S. A. Worcester secretary.

The meeting was opened with prayer by the chairman.

After deliberate consultation, the following resolutions were unanimously adopted, and ordered to be presented for publication to the editor of the Cherokee Phoenix.

Resolved, That we view the Indian Question, at present so much agitated in the United States, as being not merely of a political, but of a moral nature— inasmuch as it involves the maintenance or violation of the faith of our country —and as demanding, therefore, the most serious consideration of all American citizens, not only as patriots, but as Christians.

Resolved, That we regard the present crisis of affairs, relating to the Cherokee nation, as calling for the sympathies, and prayers, and aid, of all benevolent people throughout the United States.

Resolved, That the frequent insinuations, which have been publicly made, that missionaries have used an influence in directing the political affairs of this nation, demand from us an explicit and public disavowal of the charge; and that we therefore solemnly affirm, that in regard to ourselves at least, every such insinuation is entirely unfounded.

Resolved, That, while we distinctly aver that it is not any influence of ours, which has brought the Cherokees to the

From *The Missionary Herald,* XXVII (March, 1831), pp. 80–84.

resolution not to exchange their place of residence, yet it is impossible for us not to feel a lively interest in a subject of such vital importance to their welfare; and that we can perceive no consideration, either moral or political, which ought in the present crisis, to restrain us from a free and public expression of our opinion.

Resolved, Therefore, that we view the removal of this people to the west of the Mississippi, as an event to be most earnestly deprecated; threatening greatly to retard, if not totally to arrest their progress in religion, civilization, learning, and the useful arts; to involve them in great distress, and to bring upon them a complication of evils, for which the prospect before them would offer no compensation.

Resolved, That we deem ourselves absolutely certain that the feelings of the whole mass of the Cherokee people, including all ranks, and with scarcely a few individual exceptions, are totally averse to a removal, so that nothing but force, or such oppression as they would esteem equivalent to force, could induce them to adopt such a measure.

Resolved, As our unanimous opinion, that the establishment of the jurisdiction of Georgia and other states over the Cherokee people, against their will, would be an immense and irreparable injury.

Whereas we have frequently seen, in the public prints, representations of the state of this people, which we know to be widely at variance with the truth, and which are highly injurious to their tendency.

Resolved, That we regard it as no more than an act of justice to the Cherokee nation, that we publish the following statement, and subjoin our names in testimony of its correctness.

The Cherokee people have been advancing in civilization for a considerable number of years, and are still advancing as rapidly, we believe, as ever. Our various opportunities of acquaintance with them have been such, that we suppose our united estimate of their progress cannot vary widely from the truth. Of this, however, the public must judge. Mr. Byhan first arrived in the nation as a missionary in May 1801, left it in 1812, and returned in 1827. Mr. Butrick arrived in January and Mr. Chamberlin in March 1818. Mr. Potter and Doct. Butler arrived in January, 1821; and Mr. Elsworth and Mr. Jones in November of the same year; Mr. Proctor in October 1822; Mr. Holland in November 1823; Mr. Worcester in October 1825; Mr. Clauder in November 1828; and Mr. Thompson in January 1829. We occupy eleven stations, in different parts of the nation. One of these stations is in that part which is considered to have made the least progress of civilization.

When we say that the Cherokees are rapidly advancing in civilization, we speak of them as a body. There are very different degrees of improvement; some families having risen to a level with the white people of the United States, while the progress of others has but commenced. Between the extremes are all grades, but we do not believe there is a family in the nation, which has not in a measure felt the change. That the Indians of mixed blood should, *upon an average,* be in advance of the full Indians, was to be expected, and is undoubtedly true; although some Indians of full blood are in the foremost rank, and some of mixed blood help to bring up the rear.

It has been represented, not only that improvement is confined almost exclusively to Indians of mixed blood, but that these constitute an insignificant portion of the nation. Neither representation is correct. We believe that not less than one fourth part of the people are in a greater or less degree mixed. The number of families of mixed blood has been stated at about two hundred, which is less than the number of families of which one parent is white. That these can bear but a small proportion to the number in which one or both parents are of mixed blood is manifest, since the process of amalgamation has been going on for many years, until the descendants of whites are to be found of at least the sixth generation.

But, as we have already said, it is far from being true that improvement is chiefly confined to this class. It is well known that the Cherokees were originally found by the Europeans in a purely savage state, naked almost in summer, and clothed with skins in winter, living in miserable huts, without floors or chimneys, and subsisting, partly indeed by agriculture, but mainly, by the chase. Without implements of iron, and without the art of manufacturing cloth, it could not be far otherwise. To this purely savage state the present certainly bears a far less resemblance, than to that of the civilized people of the United States. The very lowest class, with few exceptions, are, in our apprehension, as near the latter as the former. As to the straggling beggars, who are seen abroad in the white settlements, they ought only to be compared with the drunken stragglers of other nations, to judge of comparative civilization.

It would swell our statement beyond a proper length to descend into many particulars, but it seems necessary to specify a few.

At present many of the Cherokees are dressed as well as the whites around them, and of most of them the manner of dress is *substantially* the same. A part of the old men, perhaps nearly half, retain, not indeed the original Indian dress, but that, nearly, which prevailed a dozen years since. Almost all the younger men have laid it aside. A very few aged women are seen with only a petticoat and short gown, meeting each other at the waist, which, twenty years ago, was the general style of female dress. Except these very few, no woman appears without at least a decent gown, extending from the neck to the feet. Twenty years ago most of the Cherokee children, of both sexes, were entirely naked during most of the year. Now there are few, if any families, where the children are not habitually clothed; and especially a Cherokee girl, without decent clothing, is an object very seldom seen. If the present course continues, when those who are now in the decline of life shall have passed away, the dress of the Cherokees will scarcely distinguish them from their white neighbors.

The Cherokee women generally manufacture more or less good substantial cloth. Many families raise their own cotton. A great part of their clothing is manufactured by themselves, though not a little is of New England and foreign manufacture.

Thirty years ago a plough was scarcely seen in the nation. Twenty years ago there were nearly 500. Still the ground was cultivated chiefly by the hoe only. Six years ago the number of ploughs, as enumerated, was 2,923. Among us all, we scarcely know a field which is now cultivated without ploughing. Consequently the quantity of land under cultivation is increased several fold. Habits of industry are much increased, and still increasing; and though many fail in this respect, so that the more indolent sometimes trespass upon the hospitality of the more industrious, yet most families provide, in the produce of their fields, for the supply of their own wants, and many raise considerable quantities of corn for sale. Suffering for want of food is as rare, we believe, as in any part of the civilized world.

The dwellings of the mass of the Cherokees are comfortable log cabins. The meanest are not meaner than those of some of the neighboring whites. Formerly their huts had neither floors nor chimneys. Twenty years since nearly all had chimneys, but few had floors. Now most of the cabins are floored, besides being much improved in other respects. Many of the houses in the nation are decent two story buildings, and some are elegant.

In the furniture of their houses, perhaps, the mass of the people suffer more, than in almost any other respect, by comparison with their white neighbors. Yet in this particular we notice a very rapid change in the course of a few years past.

The diffusion of property among the people is becoming more general.

In no respect, perhaps, is the approach to civilization more evident than in regard to the station assigned to women. Though in this respect there is still room for improvement, yet in general they are allowed to hold their proper place.

Polygamy, which has prevailed to some extent, is becoming rare. It is forbidden by law, but the law being as yet without a penalty annexed, has probably much less influence than public opinion, which makes the practice highly disreputable. A few are still living in a state of polygamy, but at present almost no one enters the state.

Superstition still bears considerable sway, but its influence is rapidly declining. Customs which once it was infamous to violate are fast disappearing. Most of the young men of the nation appear to be entirely ignorant of a large portion of the former superstitions. Ancient traditions are fading from memory, and can scarcely be collected, if any one would commit them to paper. Conjuring, however, is still, to a considerable extent, practised by the old, and believed in by the less enlightened even of the young.

In regard to intemperance there is much to deplore, but it is, we believe, an undisputed fact, that its prevalence has greatly diminished, and is still diminishing. Indeed we are confident that, at present, the Cherokees would not suffer in this respect by a comparison with the white population around. In regard to the scenes of intoxication exhibited at the sessions of courts, and on other public occasions, the Cherokees, in consequence of their wholesome laws on the subject, have greatly the advantage.

In education we do not know that the progress of the Cherokees should be called rapid. Certainly it is far less so than is desirable. The following facts, however, will serve to correct some misstatements on this subject. We have before us the names of 200 Cherokee men and youths who are believed to have obtained an English education sufficient for the transaction of ordinary business. Females, it will be observed, are excluded, as are many men and youths who can barely read and write. Of these 200 persons, about 132 were instructed wholly within the nation, about 24 received within the nation sufficient instruction to enable them to transact ordinary business, independently of superadded advantages, and about 44 were instructed chiefly abroad. We doubt not that a more extended acquaintance would increase the list. An increasing anxiety among the people for the education of their children is very apparent.

Of the number who are able to read their own language in Guess's alphabet we should vary somewhat in our individual estimates. None of us, however, supposes that less than a majority of those who are between childhood and middle age can read with greater or less facility.

Nothing could be further from the truth than the representation that any class of the Cherokees are in any respect deteriorating. However slow may be the progress of a portion of the people, their course is manifestly not retrograde, but progressive.

In regard to the state of religion we deem it sufficient to state, as nearly as we are able, the number of members of the several religious societies. To the Presbyterian churches belong 219 members, of whom 167 are Cherokees. In the United Brethren's churches are 45 Cherokee members. In the Baptist churches probably about 90; we know not the exact number. The official statement of the Methodist missionaries made a little more than a year ago gave 736 as the number of members in their societies, including those who are denominated seekers. The number according to the report of the present year we have not been able to ascertain. We are assured not less than 850. Of these the greater part are Cherokees.

While we represent the Cherokee people as having made great advances in civilization and knowledge, as well as in religion, we wish not to be understood to attribute all to the influence of missionary efforts. We trust indeed that missionaries, besides introducing the religion of the gospel, have had their share of influence in promoting education and the habits of civilized life. But this influence has not been alone, nor was it the first which began to be felt.

The intermixture of white people with the Indians has undoubtedly been a considerable cause of the civilization of the latter. The operation of this cause upon the descendants of white men we believe is not called in question; but some have seemed to suppose its influence on the full Indians to have been of an opposite character. To say nothing of the improbability of such a supposition considered as theory, it is manifestly contrary to fact in relation to this people. The less civilized Indians are led by degrees, and more and more rapidly, as prejudices subside, to adopt the better customs of the more civilized, whose examples are constantly before them.

The proximity of the whites, also, is by no means injurious in every respect. The evil which they have brought upon the Indians by the introduction of ardent spirits, and of vices before unknown among them, is indeed great. On the other hand, however, the gradual assimilation of the tribe, thus surrounded by civilized people, to the customs and manners which constantly invite their imitation, and the facility thus afforded for procuring the comforts of life, are benefits of no little value. To deprive them of these advantages, while in their present state, would be an incalculable evil.

In relation to the arts of civilized life, and especially those of spinning and weaving, most important results were produced by the system of means proposed by Washington, and carried into effect by some of the former agents of the government; particularly Col. Dinsmore, to whom the Cherokees acknowledge themselves greatly indebted.

It has been often represented that white men and half-breeds control the political affairs of the nation. White men can, by the constitution, have no part in the government; and to us it is evident that the influence of the white citizens of the nation over its political concerns is of very little consideration. For ourselves we have already disclaimed such influence. Not only have we been disposed, on our own part, carefully to avoid all interference with such concerns, but we well know that the Cherokees would ever have repelled such interference with indignation. Since, however, all that has been said of our influence has been mere surmise, without even the pretence of evidence, we cannot suppose that much more is necessary on our part, than to deny the charge.

That the Indians of mixed blood possess, in a considerable degree, that superior influence which naturally attends superior knowledge, cannot be doubted. Of this description certainly are the greater portion of those through whose influence a happier form of government has taken the place of that under which the Cherokees formerly lived. But it would be a power of a far different kind from any which exists in the Cherokee nation, which could, as these leading men have been represented to do, assume and maintain an important position, in opposition to the will of the people. Particularly is there overwhelming evidence, that no man, whatever degree of talent, or knowledge, or previous influence he might possess, could possibly find his way into office at the present time, whose views were known to contravene those of the mass of the people on the grand subject of national interest—a removal to the west. The disposal of office is in the hands of the people—the people require patriotism, and the very touchstone of patriotism is, "Will he sell his country?"

It may not be amiss to state what proportion the Indian blood actually bears to the white in the principal departments of the Cherokee government. The present principal chief, Mr. John Ross, is, we believe, but one eighth Cherokee. Maj. Lowrey, the second principal chief, is one half Cherokee. The legislature consists of two branches, styled the National Committee and Council, the former numbering 16 members and the latter 24. The presiding officers of both these branches are full Cherokees. Of the committee two only, including the president, are full Indians, of the rest, seven are half Indian, two more, and five less, than half. Of the Council, 16 are supposed to be full Indians, seven half, and one only one fourth. No measure can be adopted without the concurrence of both houses, and consequently every public measure has the sanction of a body of which two thirds of the members are of unmixed Indian blood. Each succeeding election may vary the proportion. This is, as nearly as we can ascertain, the proportion as it now stands.

The effect of the new form of government, adopted by the Cherokees, has been represented abroad, we know not on what grounds, to be prejudicial to the interests of the people. On this subject it does not belong to us to theorize. We can only say that the actual effect, as it passes under our own observation, is highly beneficial; nor is there any class on whom it operates injuriously.

One other representation we feel it our duty to notice, viz: that the people are deterred from the expression of opinion by the fear of the chiefs. Nothing, we are sure, could be more unfounded. Freedom of speech exists nowhere more unrestrained than here. Individuals may very possibly be restrained from the expression of an opinion favorable to the removal of the nation, by the dread of incurring the odium of public sentiment; but this is the only restraint, and it is one which supposes, what in fact exists, an overwhelming torrent of national feeling in opposition to removal.

It is on this subject, most of all, that the views of the Cherokees have been ascribed to the influence of missionaries. In denying all interference with their political concerns, we have repelled this insinuation. We would not be understood to affirm that we have always studiously avoided the expression of our opinions, but that we have not acted the part of advisers, nor would, nor could have influenced the views of the people or of their rulers.

In reference to the subjecting of the Cherokees to the jurisdiction of the several states, whose chartered limits embrace their country, it may not be improper to state what, from a constant residence among them, we cannot but perceive to be their feelings. One sentiment manifestly pervades the whole nation—that the extension of the laws of the states over them, without their consent, would be a most oppressive and flagrant violation of their natural and conventional rights; and the sufferance of it by the United States, as flagrant a violation of those treaties on which alone they have relied for security. It would

be as idle, also, as it is distant from our wish, to conceal, that our views on this subject accord with theirs, and that on a topic of such universal excitement, it is impossible that our views should be unknown to them. If the free expression of such an opinion be a crime, to the charge of that crime we plead guilty. If we withheld our opinion when called for, we could not hold up our heads as preachers of righteousness among a people who would universally regard us as abettors of iniquity.

While such are the feelings of the Cherokees, it is impossible that the jurisdiction of the several states should be established over them without producing the most unhappy results. It is not easy to conjecture what course, in such an event, the majority would adopt. Any thing approaching to unanimity could not be expected. Some would undoubtedly join their brethren in Arkansas; some, if we may judge from remarks which we frequently hear, would seek a refuge beyond the boundaries of the United States; while others still would make the experiment of remaining, subject to authorities to which they must render an unwilling obedience. Either alternative would be adopted with such feelings as would in many, we fear in most instances, preclude the probability of their making further progress in improvement, or even retaining the ground they have gained. The news of the failure of their cause, would drive them to despair, and despair, there is every reason to fear, would goad many of them on to ruinous excesses of vice, if not, in some instances, to blind revenge. Hard is the task of that philanthropist who would attempt to elevate, or even to sustain the character of a broken-hearted people.—But we forbear to dwell upon the anticipation of evils which we earnestly hope will never be realized.

In all the preceding statements we are conscious of having honestly endeavored to avoid every degree of exaggeration. To us it appears that the Cherokees are in a course of improvement, which promises, if uninterrupted, to place them, at no distant period, nearly on a level with their white brethren. Laboring, as we are, to aid them in their progress, we cannot do otherwise than earnestly deprecate any measure which threatens to arrest it. In this light we view the attempt to remove them from their inheritance, or subject them, against their will, to the dominion of others. Our sympathies are with them—our prayers have often ascended, and shall still ascend in their behalf—and we earnestly invite the prayers of all our fellow Christians, that HE who rules the destinies of nations will deliver them out of all their afflictions, and establish them in the land which he has given them; and at the same time, that he will open all their hearts to receive the gospel of his Son, and thus to secure to themselves the possession of a better country, even a heavenly.   (*Signed,*)

Gottlieb Byhan, D. S. Butrick, Wm. Chamberlin, Evan Jones, Wm. Potter, S. A. Worcester, John Thompson, H. G. Clauder, Isaac Proctor, J. C. Elsworth, E. Butler, Wm. Holland.

John Marshall:
THE CHEROKEE NATION *VS.*
THE STATE OF GEORGIA

As the removal bill became law, as the State of Georgia proclaimed its sovereignty over the territory of the Cherokee nation, the chiefs of the nation, led by John Ross, turned to the Supreme Court for the relief which they could not obtain from President Jackson. They had good reason to expect that John Marshall would give them a favorable hearing. Although he had been born in a log cabin on the Virginia frontier, although he was largely self-educated (his legal training was informal except for a series of lectures given, at William and Mary, by the eminent chancellor, George Wythe), John Marshall was quite unlike Andrew Jackson. Marshall had, for thirty years, dominated the Supreme Court. In decision after decision, he asserted the right of judicial review. In case after case, he maintained the Federalist's determination to protect the rights of property. Moreover, Marshall disliked Jackson and had, in 1828, dropped the mantle of judicial impartiality in order to campaign against Jackson's election to the presidency. The Cherokees were hopeful.

THIS bill is brought by the Cherokee nation, praying an injunction to restrain the state of Georgia from execution of certain laws of that state, which, as is alleged, go directly to annihilate the Cherokees as a political society, and to seize, for the use of Georgia, the lands of the nation which have been assured to them by the United States in solemn treaties repeatedly made and still in force.

If courts were permitted to indulge their sympathies, a case better calculated to excite them can scarcely be imagined.

A people once numerous, powerful, and truly independent, found by our ancestors in the quiet and uncontrolled possession of an ample domain, gradually sinking beneath our superior policy, our arts and our arms, have yielded their lands by successive treaties, each of which contains a solemn guarantee of the residue, until they retain no more of their formerly extensive territory than is deemed necessary to their comfortable subsistence. To preserve this remnant, the present application is made.

Before we can look into the merits of

John Marshall, "The Cherokee Nation *vs.* The State of Georgia," from *Peters Reports*, V, 75–20.

the case, a preliminary inquiry presents itself. Has this court jurisdiction of the cause?

The third article of the constitution describes the extent of the judicial power. The second section closes an enumeration of the cases to which it is extended, with "controversies" "between a state or the citizens thereof, and foreign states, citizens, or subjects." A subsequent clause of the same section gives the supreme court original jurisdiction in all cases in which a state shall be a party. The party defendant may then unquestionably be sued in this court. May the plaintiff sue in it? Is the Cherokee nation a foreign state in the sense in which that term is used in the constitution?

The counsel for the plaintiffs have maintained the affirmative of this proposition with great earnestness and ability. So much of the argument as was intended to prove the character of the Cherokees as a state, as a distinct political society, separated from others, capable of managing its own affairs and governing itself, has, in the opinion of a majority of the judges, been completely successful. They have been uniformly treated as a state from the settlement of our country. The numerous treaties made with them by the United States recognize them as a people capable of maintaining the relations of peace and war, of being responsible in their political character for any violation of their engagements, or for any aggression committed on the citizens of the United States by any individual of their community. Laws have been enacted in the spirit of these treaties. The acts of our government plainly recognize the Cherokee nation as a state, and courts are bound by those acts.

A question of much more difficulty remains. Do the Cherokees constitute a foreign state in the sense of the constitution?

The counsel have shown conclusively that they are not a state of the union, and have insisted that individually they are aliens, not owing allegiance to the United States. An aggregate of aliens composing a state must, they say, be a foreign state. Each individual being foreign, the whole must be foreign.

This argument is imposing, but we must examine it more closely before we yield to it. The condition of the Indians in relation to the United States is perhaps unlike that of any other two people in existence. In the general, nations not owing a common allegiance are foreign to each other. The term *foreign nation* is, with strict propriety, applicable by either to the other. But the relation of the Indians to the United States is marked by peculiar and cardinal distinctions which exist no where else.

The Indian territory is admitted to compose a part of the United States. In all our maps, geographical treatises, histories, and laws, it is so considered. In all our intercourse with foreign nations, in our commercial regulations, in any attempt at intercourse between Indians and foreign nations, they are considered as within the jurisdictional limits of the United States, subject to many of those restraints which are imposed upon our own citizens. They acknowledge themselves in their treaties to be under the protection of the United States; they admit that the United States shall have the sole and exclusive right of regulating the trade with them, and managing all their affairs as they think proper; and the Cherokees in particular were allowed by the treaty of Hopewell, which preceded the constitution, "to send a deputy of their choice, whenever they think fit, to congress." Treaties were made with some tribes by the state of New York, under a then unsettled construction of the confederation, by which they ceded all their lands to that state, taking back a limited grant to themselves, in which they admit their dependence.

Though the Indians are acknowledged to have an unquestionable, and, heretofore, unquestioned right to the lands they occupy, until that right shall be extinguished by a voluntary cession to our government; yet it may well be doubted whether those tribes which reside within the acknowledged boundaries of the United States can, with strict accuracy, be denominated foreign nations. They may, more correctly, perhaps, be denominated domestic dependent nations. They occupy a territory to which we assert a title independent of their will, which must take effect in point of possession when their right of possession ceases. Meanwhile they are in a state of pupilage. Their relation to the United States resembles that of a ward to his guardian.

They look to our government for protection; rely upon its kindness and its power; appeal to it for relief of their wants; and address the president as their great father. They and their country are considered by foreign nations, as well as by ourselves, as being so completely under the sovereignty and dominion of the United States, that any attempt to acquire their lands, or to form a political connexion with them, would be considered by all as an invasion of our territory, and an act of hostility.

These considerations go far to support the opinion, that the framers of our constitution had not the Indian tribes in view, when they opened the courts of the union to controversies between a state or the citizens thereof, and foreign states.

In considering this subject, the habits and usages of the Indians, in their intercourse with their white neighbors, ought not to be entirely disregarded. At the time the constitution was framed, the idea of appealing to an American court of justice for an assertion of right or a redress of wrong, had perhaps never entered the mind of an Indian or of his tribe. Their appeal was to the tomahawk, or to the government. This was well understood by the statesmen who framed the constitution of the United States, and might furnish some reason for omitting to enumerate them among the parties who might sue in the courts of the union. Be this as it may, the peculiar relations between the United States and the Indians occupying our territory are such, that we should feel much difficulty in considering them as designated by the term *foreign state*, were there no other part of the constitution which might shed light on the meaning of these words. But we think that in construing them, considerable aid is furnished by that clause in the eighth section of the third article; which empowers congress to "regulate commerce with foreign nations, and among the several states, and with the Indian tribes."

In this clause they are as clearly contradistinguished by a name appropriate to themselves, from foreign nations, as from the several states composing the union. They are designated by a distinct appellation; and as this appellation can be applied to neither of the others, neither can the appellation distinguishing either of the others be in fair construction applied to them. The objects, to which the power of regulating commerce might be directed, are divided into three distinct classes—foreign nations, the several states, and Indian tribes. When forming this article, the convention considered them as entirely distinct. We cannot assume that the distinction was lost in framing a subsequent article, unless there be something in its language to authorize the assumption.

The counsel for the plaintiffs contend that the words "Indian tribes" were introduced into the article, empowering congress to regulate commerce, for the purpose of removing those doubts in which the management of Indian affairs was involved by the language of the ninth article of the confederation. Intending to give the whole power of managing those affairs to the government about to be instituted, the convention conferred it explicitly; and omitted those qualifications which embarrassed the exercise of it as granted in the confederation. This may be admitted without weakening the construction which has been intimated. Had the Indian tribes been foreign nations, in the view of the convention, this exclusive power of regulating intercourse with them might have been, and most probably would have been, specifically given, in language indicating that idea, not in language contradistinguishing them from foreign nations. Congress might have been empowered "to regulate commerce with foreign nations, including the Indian tribes, and among the several states." This language would have suggested itself to statesmen who considered the Indian tribes as foreign nations, and were yet desirous of mentioning them particularly.

It has been also said, that the same words have not necessarily the same meaning attached to them when found in different parts of the same instrument; their meaning is controlled by the context. This is undoubtedly true. In common language the same word has various meanings, and the peculiar sense in which it is used in any sentence is to be determined by the context. This may not be equally true with respect to proper names. *Foreign nations* is a general term, the application of which to Indian tribes, when used in the American constitution, is at best extremely questionable. In one article in which a power is given to be exercised in regard to foreign nations generally, and to the Indian tribes particularly, they are mentioned as separate in terms clearly contradistinguishing them from each other. We perceive plainly that the constitution in this article does not comprehend Indian tribes in the general term "foreign nations"; not we presume because a tribe may not be a nation, but because it is not foreign to the United States. When, afterwards, the term "foreign state" is introduced, we cannot impute to the convention the intention to desert its former meaning, and to comprehend Indian tribes within it, unless the context force that construction on us. We find nothing in the context, and nothing in the subject of the article, which leads to it.

The court has bestowed its best attention on this question, and, after mature deliberation, the majority is of opinion that an Indian tribe or nation within the United States is not a foreign state in the sense of the constitution, and cannot maintain an action in the courts of the United States.

A serious additional objection exists to the jurisdiction of the court. Is the matter of the bill the proper subject for judicial inquiry and decision? It seeks to restrain a state from the forcible exercise of legislative power over a neighbouring people, asserting their independence; their right to which the state denies. On several of the matters alleged in the bill, for example on the laws making it criminal to exercise the usual powers of self-government in their own country by the Cherokee nation, this court cannot interpose; at least in the form in which those matters are presented.

That part of the bill which respects the land occupied by the Indians, and prays the aid of the court to protect their possession, may be more doubtful. The mere question of right might perhaps be decided by this court in a proper case with proper parties. But the court is asked to do more than decide on the title. The bill requires us to control the legislature of Georgia, and to restrain the exertion of its physical force. The propriety of such an interposition by the court may be well questioned. It savours too much of the exercise of political power to be within the proper province of the judicial department. But the opinion on the point respecting parties makes it unnecessary to decide this question.

If it be true that the Cherokee nation have rights, this is not the tribunal in which those rights are to be asserted. If it be true that wrongs have been inflicted, and that still greater are to be apprehended, this is not the tribunal which can redress the past or prevent the future.

The motion for an injunction is denied.

Smith Thompson:

THE CHEROKEE NATION VS.
THE STATE OF GEORGIA:
DISSENTING OPINION

Although Justices William Johnson and Henry Baldwin concurred
with Marshall, Justice Thompson dissented, and was joined in his
dissent by Justice Story. Thompson, who wrote the dissenting opinion,
was a Jeffersonian who had left the New York Supreme Court (on
which he served from 1802 to 1818) in order to become President
Monroe's Secretary of the Navy. Although he was an Associate Justice
of the Supreme Court from 1823, Thompson angered the Jacksonians
by running against Van Buren for the governorship of New York. He
frequently disagreed with Marshall's opinions. Justice Joseph Story,
who concurred with Thompson, was, on the other hand, Marshall's
closest associate on the court; Story's concurrence with Thompson is
thought by some historians to have influenced Marshall's opinion in
the case of Worcester vs. Georgia.

IT is a rule which has been repeatedly sanctioned by this court, that the judicial department is to consider as sovereign and independent states or nations those powers, that are recognized as such by the executive and legislative departments of the government; they being more particularly entrusted with our foreign relations. . . . If we look to the whole course of treatment by this country of the Indians, from the year 1775, to the present day, when dealing with them in their aggregate capacity as nations or tribes, and regarding the mode and manner in which all negotiations have been carried on and concluded with them; the conclusion appears to me irresistible, that they have been regarded, by the executive and legislative branches of the government, not only as sovereign and independent, but as foreign nations or tribes, not within the jurisdiction nor under the government of the states within which they were located. . . . Other departments of the government, whose right it is to decide what powers shall be recognized as sovereign and independent nations, have treated [the Cherokee Nation] as such. They have considered it competent, in its political and national capacity, to enter into contracts of the most solemn

Smith Thompson, "The Cherokee Nation *vs.* The State of Georgia," from *Peters Reports*, V, 59–80.

character; and if these contracts contain matter proper for judicial inquiry, why should we refuse to entertain jurisdiction of the case? Such jurisdiction is expressly given to this court in cases arising under treaties. If the executive department does not think proper to enter into treaties or contracts with the Indian nations, no case with them can arise calling for judicial cognizance. But when such treaties are found containing stipulations proper for judicial cognizance, I am unable to discover any reasons satisfying my mind that this court has not jurisdiction of the case.

The next inquiry is, whether such a case is made out in the bill as to warrant this court in granting any relief?

I have endeavoured to show that the Cherokee nation is a foreign state; and, as such, a competent party to maintain an original suit in this court against one of the United States. The injuries complained of are violations committed and threatened upon the property of the complainants, secured to them by the laws and treaties of the United States. Under the constitution, the judicial power of the United States extends expressly to all cases in law and equity, arising under the laws of the United States, and treaties made or which shall be made, under the authority of the same. . . .

[Justice Thompson then examined the treaties of Hopewell and Holston and the Act of 1802, "An act to regulate trade and intercourse with the Indian tribes, and to preserve peace on the frontiers." Justice Thompson concluded that this act and the aforementioned treaties did guarantee the Cherokee nation the rights which the nation claimed in its appeal to the Court.]

These treaties are acknowledged by the United States to be in full force, by the proviso to the seventh section of the act of the 28th May 1830; which declares, that nothing in this act contained shall be construed as authorising or directing the violation of any existing treaty between the United States and any Indian tribes.

That the Cherokee nation of Indians have, by virtue of these treaties, an exclusive right of occupancy of the lands in question, and that the United States are bound under their guarantee, to protect the nation in the enjoyment of such occupancy; cannot, in my judgment, admit of a doubt: and that some of the laws of Georgia set out in the bill are in violation of, and in conflict with those treaties and the act of 1802, is to my mind equally clear. . . .

[Justice Thompson then specified the Georgia laws which violated the provisions of the various treaties.]

These instances are sufficient to show a direct, and palpable infringement of the rights of property secured to the complainants by treaty, and in violation of the act of congress of 1802. These treaties and this law, are declared by the constitution to be the supreme law of the land: it follows, as a matter of course, that the laws of Georgia, so far as they are repugnant to them, must be void and inoperative. And it remains only very briefly to inquire whether the execution of them can be restrained by injunction according to the doctrine and practice of courts of equity. . . . The doctrine of this court in the case of Osborne vs. The United States Bank . . . fully sustains the present application for an injunction. . . . The laws of the state of Georgia in this case go as fully to the total destruction of the complainants' rights as did the law of Ohio to the destruction of the rights of the bank in that state; and an injunction is as fit and proper in this case to prevent the injury, as it was in that. . . .

Upon the whole, I am of [the] opinion,

1. That the Cherokees compose a foreign state within the sense and meaning of the constitution, and constitute a competent party to maintain a suit against the state of Georgia.

2. That the bill presents a case for judicial consideration, arising under the laws of the United States, and treaties made under their authority with the Cherokee nation, and which laws and treaties have been, and are threatened to be still further violated by the laws of the state of Georgia referred to in this opinion.

3. That an injunction is a fit and proper writ to be issued, to prevent the further execution of such laws, and ought therefore to be awarded.

John Marshall:

WORCESTER *VS.* THE
STATE OF GEORGIA

Shortly after the meeting of the missionaries on December 29, 1830, the Georgia guard entered the Cherokee territory and, under provisions of the Georgia Law of December 22, 1830, arrested a number of missionaries for residing in the Cherokee territory without a license from the State of Georgia. The Superior Court of Gwinnett County, Judge Augustin S. Clayton presiding, released the missionaries upon the ground that they were, as missionaries, agents of the United States. However, when Governor Gilmer inquired about this, President Jackson informed him that the men, except for the Rev. Samuel Worcester, were not United States agents. Moreover, Worcester, who was United States postmaster at New Echota, was removed from that office by President Jackson and, subsequently, arrested once again, tried, and found guilty. The case was appealed to the United States Supreme Court. Once again, John Marshall rendered the majority opinion.

THIS cause, in every point of view in which it can be placed, is of the deepest interest.

The defendant is a state, a member of the union, which has exercised the powers of government over a people who deny its jurisdiction, and are under the protection of the United States.

The plaintiff is a citizen of the state of Vermont, condemned to hard labour for four years in the penitentiary of Georgia; under colour of an act which he alleges to be repugnant to the Constitution, laws, and treaties of the United States.

The legislative power of a state, the controlling power of the Constitution and laws of the United States, the rights, if they have any, the political existence of a once numerous and powerful people, the personal liberty of a citizen, are all involved in the subject now to be considered.

It behooves this court, in every case, more especially in this, to examine into its jurisdiction with scrutinizing eyes; before it proceeds to the exercise of a power which is controverted.

The first step in the performance of this duty is the inquiry whether the record is properly before the court.

It is certified by the clerk of the court, which pronounced the judgment of condemnation under which the plaintiff in error is imprisoned; and is also authenti-

From *Peters Reports*, VI, 536–563.

cated by the seal of the court. It is returned with, and annexed to, a writ of error issued in regular form, the citation being signed by one of the associate justices of the supreme court, and served on the governor and attorney-general of the state, more than thirty days before the commencement of the term to which the writ of error was returnable.

The judicial act [of 1789], so far as it prescribes the mode of proceeding, appears to have been literally pursued. . . .

The record, then, according to the judiciary act, and the rule and the practice of the court, is regularly before us. The more important inquiry is, does it exhibit a case cognizable by this tribunal?

The indictment charges the plaintiff in error, and others, being white persons, with the offence of "residing within the limits of the Cherokee nation without a license," and "without having taken the oath to support and defend the constitution and laws of the state of Georgia."

The defendant in the state court appeared in proper person, and [pled that the laws under which he had been indicted were contrary to treaties "which, according to the Constitution of the United States, compose a part of the supreme law of the land," contrary to Article I, Section 8, of the Constitution, and, in addition, contrary to Federal laws regulating trade and intercourse with the various Indian tribes].

This plea was overruled by the court [of the state of Georgia]. And the prisoner, being arraigned, pled not guilty. The jury found a verdict against him, and the court sentenced him to hard labour, in the penitentiary, for the term of four years.

By overruling this plea, the court decided that the matter it contained was not a bar to the action. The plea, there-fore, must be examined, for the purpose of determining whether it makes a case which brings the party within the provisions of the twenty-fifth section of the "act to establish the judicial courts of the United States."

The plea avers, that the residence, charged in the indictment, was under the authority of the President of the United States, and with the permission and approval of the Cherokee nation. That the treaties, subsisting between the United States and the Cherokees, acknowledge their right as a sovereign nation to govern themselves and all persons who have settled within their territory, free from any right of legislative interference by the several states composing the United States of America. That the act under which the prosecution was instituted is repugnant to the said treaties, and is, therefore, unconstitutional and void. That the said act is, also, unconstitutional; because it interferes with, and attempts to regulate and control, the intercourse with the Cherokee nation, which belongs, exclusively, to Congress; and, because, also, it is repugnant to the statute of the United States, entitled "an act to regulate trade and intercourse with the Indian tribes, and to preserve peace on the frontiers."

Let the averments of this plea be compared with the twenty-fifth section of the judicial act [of 1789].

That section enumerates the cases in which the final judgment or decree of a state court may be revised in the Supreme Court of the United States. These are, "where is drawn in question the validity of a treaty, or statute of, or an authority exercised under, the United States, and the decision is against their validity; or where is drawn in question the validity of a statute of, or an authority exercised under any state, on the ground of their being repugnant to the constitution, treaties or laws of the United States, and the decision is in favour of such their validity; or where is drawn in question the construction of any clause of the constitution, or of a treaty, or statute of, or commission held under the United States, and the decision is against the title, right, privilege or exemption, specially set up or claimed by either party under such clause of the said constitution, treaty, statute or commission."

The indictment and plea in this case draw in question, we think, the validity of the treaties made by the United States with the Cherokee Indians; if not so, their construction is certainly drawn in question; and the decision has been, if not against their validity, "against the right, privilege or exemption, specially set up and claimed under them." They also draw into question the validity of a statute of the state of Georgia, "on the ground of its being repugnant to the Constitution, treaties and laws of the United States, and the decision is in favour of its validity."

It is, then, we think, too clear for controversy, that the act of Congress, by which this court is constituted, has given it the power, and of course imposed on it the duty, of exercising jurisdiction in this case. This duty, however unpleasant, cannot be avoided. Those who fill the judicial department have no discretion in selecting the subjects to be brought before them. We must examine the defence set up in this plea. We must inquire and decide whether the act of the legislature of Georgia, under which the plaintiff in error has been prosecuted and condemned, be consistent with, or repugnant to, the constitution, laws and treaties of the United States. . . .

During the war of the revolution, the Cherokees took part with the British. After its termination, the United States, though desirous of peace, did not feel its necessity so strongly as while the war continued. Their political situation being changed, they might very well think it advisable to assume a higher tone, and to impress on the Cherokees the same respect for congress which was before felt for the king of Great Britain. This may account for the language of the Treaty of Hopewell. There is the more reason for supposing that the Cherokee chiefs were not very critical judges of the language, from the fact that every one makes his mark; no chief was capable of signing his name. It is probable that the treaty was interpreted to them.

The treaty is introduced with the declaration, that "the commissioners plenipotentiary of the United States give peace to all the Cherokees, and receive them into the favour and protection of the United States of America, on the following conditions."

When the United States gave peace, did they not also receive it? Were not both parties desirous of it? If we consult the history of the day, does it not inform us that the United States were at least as anxious to obtain it as the Cherokees? We may ask, further: did the Cherokees come to the seat of the American government to solicit peace; or, did the American commissioners go to them to obtain it? The treaty was made at Hopewell, not at New York. The word "give," then, has no real importance attached to it.

The first and second articles stipulate for the mutual restoration of prisoners, and are of course equal.

The third article acknowledges the Cherokees to be under the protection of the United States of America, and of no other power.

This stipulation is found in Indian treaties, generally. It was introduced into their treaties with Great Britain; and may probably be found in those with other European powers. Its origin may be traced to the nature of their connexion with those powers; and its true meaning is discerned in their relative situation.

The general law of European sovereigns, respecting their claims in America, limited the intercourse of Indians, in a great degree, to the particular potentate whose ultimate right of domain was acknowledged by the others. This was the general state of things in time of peace. It was sometimes changed in war. The consequence was, that their supplies were derived chiefly from that nation, and their trade confined to it. Goods, indispensable to their comfort, in the shape of presents, were received from the same hand. What was of still more importance, the strong hand of government was interposed to restrain the disorderly and licentious from intrusions into their country, from encroachments on their lands, and from those acts of violence which were often attended by reciprocal murder. The Indians perceived in this protection only what was beneficial to themselves—an engagement to punish aggressions on them. It involved, practically, no claim to their lands, no dominion over their persons. It merely bound the nation to the British crown, as a dependent ally, claiming the protection of a powerful friend and neighbor, and receiving the advantages of that protection, without involving a surrender of their national character.

This is the true meaning of the stipulation, and is undoubtedly the sense in which it was made. Neither the British government, nor the Cherokees, ever understood it otherwise.

The same stipulation entered into with the United States, is undoubtedly to be construed in the same manner. They receive the Cherokee nation into their favour and protection. The Cherokees acknowledge themselves to be under the protection of the United States, and of no other power. Protection does not imply the destruction of the protected. The manner in which this stipulation was understood by the American government, is explained by the language and acts of our first president.

The fourth article draws the boundary between the Indians and the citizens of the United States. But, in describing this boundary, the term "allotted" and the term "hunting ground" are used.

Is it reasonable to suppose, that the Indians, who could not write, and most probably could not read, who certainly were not critical judges of our language, should distinguish the word "allotted" from the words "marked out"[?] The actual subject of contract was the dividing line between the two nations, and their attention may very well be supposed to have been confined to that subject. When, in fact, they were ceding lands to the United States, and describing the extent of their cession, it may very well be supposed that they might not understand the term employed, as indicating that, instead of granting, they were receiving lands. If the term would admit of no other signification, which is not conceded, its being misunderstood is so apparent, results so necessarily from the whole transaction; that it must, we think, be taken in the sense in which it was most obviously used.

So with respect to the words "hunting grounds." Hunting was at that time the principal occupation of the Indians, and their land was more used for that purpose than for any other. It could not, however, be supposed, that any intention existed of restricting the full use of the lands they reserved. . . .

The fifth article withdraws the protection of the United States from any citizen who has settled, or shall settle, on the lands allotted to the Indians, for their hunting grounds; and stipulates that, if he shall not remove within six months the Indians may punish him.

The sixth and seventh articles stipulate for the punishment of the citizens of either country, who may commit offenses on or against the citizens of the other. The only inference to be drawn from them is, that the United States considered the Cherokees as a nation.

The ninth article is in these words: "for the benefit and comfort of the Indians, and for the prevention of injuries or oppressions on the part of the citizens or Indians, the United States, in Congress assembled, shall have the sole and exclusive right of regulating the trade with the Indians, and *managing all their affairs,* as they think proper."

To construe the expression "managing all their affairs," into a surrender of self-government, would be, we think, a perversion of their necessary meaning, and a departure from the construction which has been uniformly put on them. The great subject of the article is the Indian trade. The influence it gave, made it desirable that Congress should possess it. The commissioners brought forward the claim, with the profession that their motive was "the benefit and comfort of the Indians, and the prevention of injuries or oppressions." This may be true, as respects the regulation of their trade, and as respects the regulation of all affairs connected with their trade, but cannot be true, as respects the management of all their affairs. The most important of these, are the cession of their lands, and security against intruders on them. Is it credible, that they should have considered themselves as surrendering to the United States the right to dictate their future cessions, and the terms on which they should be made? or to compel their submission to the violence of disorderly and licentious intruders? It is equally inconceivable that they could have supposed themselves, by a phrase thus slipped into an article, on another and most interesting subject, to have divested themselves of the right of self-government on subjects not connected with trade. Such a measure could not be "for their benefit and comfort," or for "the injuries and oppression." Such a construction would be inconsistent with the spirit of this and of all subsequent treaties; especially of those articles which recognise the right of the Cherokees to declare hostilities, and to make war. It would convert a treaty of peace covertly into an act, annihilating the political existence of one of the parties. Had such a result been intended, it would have been openly avowed. . . .

The Treaty of Hopewell seems not to have established a solid peace. To accommodate the differences still existing between the state of Georgia and the Cherokee nation, the Treaty of Holston was negotiated in July 1791. The existing Constitution of the United States had been then adopted, and the government, having more intrinsic capacity to enforce its just claims, was perhaps less mindful of high sounding expressions, denoting superiority. We hear no more of giving peace to the Cherokees. The mutual desire of establishing permanent peace and friendship, and of removing all causes of war, is honestly avowed, and, in pursuance of this desire, the first article declares, that there shall be perpetual peace and friendship between all the citizens of the United States of America and all the individuals composing the Cherokee nation.

The second article repeats the important acknowledgement, that the Cherokee nation is under the protection of the United States of America, and of no other sovereign whomsoever.

The meaning of this has been already explained. . . . This relation was that of a nation claiming and receiving the protection of one more powerful: not that of individuals abandoning their national character, and submitting as subjects to the laws of a master.

The third article contains a perfectly equal stipulation for the surrender of prisoners.

The fourth article declares, that "the boundary between the United States and the Cherokee nation shall be as follows: beginning," etc. We hear no more of "allotments" or of "hunting grounds." A boundary is described, between nation and nation, by mutual consent. The national character of each; the ability of each to establish this boundary, is acknowledged by the other. To preclude for ever all disputes, it is agreed that it shall be plainly marked by commissioners, to be appointed by each party; and, in order to extinguish for ever all claim of the Cherokees to the ceded lands, an additional consideration is to be paid by the United States. For this additional consideration the Cherokees release all right to the ceded land, for ever.

By the fifth article, the Cherokees allow the United States a road through their country, and the navigation of the Tennessee River. The acceptance of these cessions is an acknowledgement of the right of the Cherokees to make or withhold them.

By the sixth article, it is agreed, on the part of the Cherokees, that the United States shall have the sole and exclusive right of regulating their trade. No claim is made to the management of all their affairs. This stipulation has already been explained. . . .

By the seventh article the United States solemnly guaranty to the Cherokee nation all their lands not hereby ceded.

The eighth article relinquishes to the Cherokees any citizens of the United States who may settle on their lands; and the ninth forbids any citizen of the United States to hunt on their lands, or to enter their country without a passport.

The remaining articles are equal, and contain stipulations which could be made only with a nation admitted to be capable of governing itself.

This treaty, thus explicitly recognizing the national character of the Cherokees, and their right of self government; thus guarantying their lands; assuming the duty of protection, and of course pledging the faith of the United States for that protection; has been frequently renewed, and is now in full force. . . .

From the commencement of our government, Congress has passed acts to regulate trade and intercourse with the Indians; which treat them as nations, respect their rights, and manifest a firm purpose to afford that protection which treaties stipulate. All these acts, and especially that of 1802, which is still in force, manifestly consider the several Indian nations as distinct political communities, having territorial boundaries, within which their authority is exclusive, and having a right to all the lands within those boundaries, which is not only acknowledged, but guarantied by the United States. . . .

The treaties and laws of the United States, [as we have seen], contemplate the Indian territory as completely separated from that of the states; and provide that all intercourse with them shall be carried on exclusively by the government of the union.

Is this the rightful exercise of power, or is it usurpation?

While these states were colonies, this power, in its utmost extent, was admitted to reside in the crown. When our revolutionary struggle commenced, Congress was composed of an assemblage of deputies acting under specific powers granted by the legislatures, or conventions of the several colonies. It was a great popular movement, not perfectly organized; nor were the respective powers of those who were entrusted with the management of affairs accurately defined. The necessities of our situation produced a general conviction that those measures which concerned all, must be transacted by a body in which the representatives of all were assembled, and which could command the confidence of all: Congress, therefore, was considered as invested with all the powers of war and peace, and Congress dissolved our connexion with the mother country, and declared these United Colonies to be independent states. . . . From the same necessity, and on the same principles, Congress assumed the management of Indian affairs. . . .

Such was the state of things when the [Articles of Confederation were] adopted. That instrument surrendered the powers of peace and war to Congress, and prohibited them to the states, respectively, unless a state be actually invaded. . . . This instrument also gave the United States in congress assembled the sole and exclusive right of "regulating the trade and managing all the affairs with the Indians, not members of any of the states: provided, that the legislative power of any state within its own limits be not infringed or violated."

The ambiguous phrases which follow the grant of power to the United States, were so construed by the states of North Carolina and Georgia as to annul the power itself. The discontents and confusion resulting from these conflicting claims, produced representations to congress, which were referred to a committee, who made their report in 1787. The report does not assent to the construction of the two states, but recommends an accommodation, by liberal cessions of territory, or by an admission, on their part, of the powers claimed by congress. The correct exposition of this article is rendered unnecessary by the adoption of our existing constitution. That instrument confers on congress the powers of war and peace; of making treaties, and of regulating commerce with foreign nations, and among the several states and *with the Indian tribes.* These powers comprehend all that is required for the regulation of our intercourse with the Indians. They are not limited by any restrictions on their free actions. The shackles imposed on this power, in the confederation, are discarded.

The Indian nations had always been considered as distinct, independent political communities, retaining their original natural rights, as the undisputed possessors of the soil, from time immemorial, with the single exception of that imposed by irresistible power, which excluded them from intercourse with any other European potentate than the first discoverer of the coast of the particular region claimed: and this was a restriction which those European potentates imposed on themselves, as well as on the Indians. The very term "nation," so generally applied to them, means "a people distinct from others." The constitution, by declaring treaties already made, as well as those to be made, to be the supreme law of the land, has adopted and sanctioned the previous treaties with the Indian nations, and consequently admits their rank among those powers who are capable of making treaties. The words "treaty" and "nation" are words of our own language, selected in our diplomatic and legislative proceedings, by ourselves, having each a definite and well understood meaning. We have applied them to Indians, as we have applied them to the other nations of the earth. They are applied to all in the same sense.

Georgia, herself, has furnished conclusive evidence that her former opinions on this subject concurred with those entertained by her sister states, and by the government of the United States. Various acts of her legislature have been cited in the argument, including the contract of cession made in the year 1802, all tending to prove her acquiescence in the universal conviction that the Indian nations possessed a full right to the lands they occupied, until that right should be extinguished by the United States, with their consent: that their territory was separated from that of any state within whose chartered limits they might reside, by a boundary line, established by treaties: that, within their boundary, they possessed rights with which no state could interfere: and that the whole power of regulating the intercourse with them, was vested in the United States. A review of these acts, on the part of Georgia, would occupy too much time, and is the less necessary, because they have been ac-

curately detailed in the argument at the bar. Her new series of laws, manifesting her abandonment of these opinions, appears to have commenced in December 1828.

In opposition to this original right, possessed by the undisputed occupants of every country; to this recognition of that right, which is evidenced by our history, in every change through which we have passed; is placed the charters granted by the monarch of a distant and distinct region, parcelling out a territory in possession of others whom he could not remove and did not attempt to remove, and the cession made of his claims by the treaty of peace.

The actual state of things at the time, and all history since, explain these charters; and the king of Great Britain, at the treaty of peace, could cede only what belonged to his crown. These newly asserted titles can derive no aid from the articles so often repeated in Indian treaties; extending to them, first, the protection of Great Britain, and afterwards that of the United States. These articles are associated with others, recognizing their title to self-government. The very fact of repeated treaties with them recognizes it; and the settled doctrine of the law of nations is, that a weaker power does not surrender its independence—its right to self-government, by associating with a stronger, and taking its protection. A weak state, in order to provide for its safety, may place itself under the protection of one more powerful, without stripping itself of the right of government, and ceasing to be a state. Examples of this kind are not wanting in Europe. "Tributary and feudatory states," says Vattel, "do not thereby cease to be sovereign and independent states, so long as self-government and sovereign and independent authority are left in the administration of the state." At the present day, more than one state may be considered as holding its right of self-government under the guarantee and protection of one or more allies.

The Cherokee nation, then, is a distinct community, occupying its own territory, with boundaries accurately described, in which the laws of Georgia can have no force, and which the citizens of Georgia have no right to enter, but with the assent of the Cherokees themselves, or in conformity with treaties, and with the acts of congress. The whole intercourse between the United States and this nation, is, by our constitution and laws, vested in the government of the United States.

The act of the state of Georgia, under which the plaintiff in error was prosecuted, is consequently void, and the judgment a nullity. Can this court revise, and reverse it?

If the objection to the system of legislation, lately adopted by the legislature of Georgia, in relation to the Cherokee nation, was confined to its extraterritorial operation, the objection, though complete, so far as respected mere right, would give this court no power over the subject. But it goes much further. If the review which has been taken be correct, and we think it is, the acts of Georgia are repugnant to the constitution, laws, and treaties of the United States.

They interfere forcibly with the relations established between the United States and the Cherokee nation, the regulation of which, according to the settled principles of our constitution, are committed exclusively to the government of the union.

They are in direct hostility with treaties, repeated in a succession of years, which mark out the boundary that separates the Cherokee country from Georgia; guaranty to them all the land within their boundary; solemnly pledge the faith of the United States to restrain their citizens from trespassing on it; and recognize the pre-existing power of the nation to govern itself.

They are in equal hostility with the acts of congress for regulating this intercourse, and giving effect to the treaties.

The forcible seizure and abduction of the plaintiff in error, who was residing in the nation with its permission, and by authority of the president of the United States, is also a violation of the acts which authorise the chief magistrate to exercise this authority.

Will these powerful considerations avail the plaintiff in error? We think they will. He was seized, and forcibly carried away, while under guardianship of treaties guarantying the country in which he resided, and taking it under the protection of the United States. He was seized while performing, under the sanction of the chief magistrate of the union, those duties which the humane policy adopted by congress had recommended. He was apprehended, tried, and condemned, under colour of a law which has been shown to be repugnant to the constitution, laws, and treaties of the United States. Had a judgment, liable to the same objections, been rendered for property, none would question the jurisdiction of this court. It cannot be less clear when the judgment affects personal liberty, and inflicts disgraceful punishment, if punishment could disgrace when inflicted on innocence. The plaintiff in error is not less interested in the operation of this unconstitutional law than if it affected his property. He is not less entitled to the protection of the constitution, laws, and treaties of his country.

The point has been elaborately argued and, after deliberate consideration, decided, in the case of Cohens v. The Commonwealth of Virginia, 6 Wheat. 264.

It is the opinion of this court that the judgment of the superior court for the county of Gwinnett, in the state of Georgia, condemning Samuel A. Worcester to hard labour, in the penitentiary of the state of Georgia, for four years, was pronounced by that court under colour of a law which is void, as being repugnant to the constitution, treaties, and laws of the United States, and ought, therefore, to be reversed and annulled.

George M. Troup:

THE SOVEREIGNTY OF THE STATES

Born near the Tombigbee River in that part of Georgia which eventually became Alabama, and educated at Princeton College, George M. Troup was the political leader of the anti-Clarke and anti-Lumpkin men in Georgia. His strongest following came from the coastal counties, from the merchants and planters. During the crisis over the removal of the Cherokees, Troup was serving as United States Senator. Since Troup, like Lumpkin, supported Andrew Jackson in the war against the rechartering of the Second Bank of the United States (and was also known as a "States' Rights Democrat"), outsiders were puzzled by the complexities of Georgia politics. ("We know not," wrote Hezekiah Niles in his Register, "what they differ about, but they do violently differ.") One thing was clear. Both factions were determined to see the final removal of the Indian tribes. Both factions were determined to carry out this policy in the face of all opposition.

Washington, 5th March, 1832.

DEAR sirs:—The people of Georgia will receive with indignant feelings, as they ought, the recent decision of the supreme court, so flagrantly violative of their sovereign rights. I hope the people will treat it, however, as becomes them; with moderation—dignity, and firmness; and so treating it, Georgia will be unhurt by what will prove it to be a *brutum fulmen*. The judges know you will not yield obedience to mandates, and they may desire *pretexts* for the enforcement of them, which I trust you will not give.

The chief magistrate of the United States will perform all his constitutional duties; but he will not lend himself to party to perform more. He will, if I mistake not, defend the sovereignty of the states, as he would the sovereignty of the union; and if the blow be aimed equally at *him* and at *us,* it would be ungenerous, by an improvident act of ours, to make him the victim of the common enemy.

The jurisdiction claimed over one portion of our population may very soon be asserted over *another;* and in both cases they will be sustained by the fanatics of the north. Very soon, therefore, things must come to their worst; and if in the last resort we need defenders, we will find them every where among the honest men of the country; whom a just and wise conduct will rally to our banner—for the rest we care nothing. Dear sirs, very respectively yours,   G. M. TROUP

George M. Troup, "The Sovereignty of the States: An Open Letter to the Georgia Journal (March 5, 1832), as printed in Niles's Register, XLII (March 31, 1832), 78.

Wilson Lumpkin:

MESSAGE TO GEORGIA LEGISLATURE

Returning from Washington to become governor (1831–1835), Wilson Lumpkin continued to work for the removal of the Cherokees. In his message to the Georgia legislature (November 6, 1832), he was able to report substantial progress and an undiminished determination.

WHEN we take a survey of the events of the closing year, it produces mingled emotions of pleasure and pain. Our actual condition and enjoyments as a people, arising from climate, soil, and good government, when compared with other portions of the world, admonish us to admire and adore the divine author of our multiplied blessings.

Nothing has transpired to lessen attachment, or diminish our confidence in the good systems of government under which we live; we should, therefore, cherish an increased zeal, and an abiding hope for the perpetuation of our free and happy institutions. The truths of history do not authorize the belief, that we are to enjoy the inestimable blessings of liberty and free government, founded on principles of equal rights, without vigilance, and constant exertion on the part of the people, who are the only legitimate source of governmental power.

Our conflicts with Federal usurpation are not yet at an end; the events of the past year have afforded us new cause for distrust and dissatisfaction. Contrary to the enlightened opinions, and just expectations of this, and every other State in the Union, a majority of the judges of the Supreme Court of the United States have not only assumed jurisdiction, in the case of Worcester and Butler, but have, by their decision, attempted to overthrow that essential jurisdiction of the State, in criminal cases, which has been vested by our constitution in the superior courts of our own state. In conformity with their decision, a mandate was issued, directed to our court, ordering a reversal of the decree under which those persons are imprisoned; thereby attempting, and intending to prostrate the sovereignty of this state in the exercise of its constitutional criminal jurisdiction. These extraordinary proceedings of the supreme court, have not been submitted to me officially, nor have they been brought before me in any manner which called for my official action. I have, however, been prepared to meet this usurpation of federal power, with the most prompt and determined resistance, in whatever

From *Niles's Register,* XLIII (November 24, 1832), 206.

form its enforcement might have been attempted, by any branch of the federal government.

It has afforded me great satisfaction to find that our whole people, as with the voice of one man, have manifested a calm, but firm and determined resolution to sustain the authorities and sovereignty of their state, against this unjust and unconstitutional encroachment of the federal judiciary. The ingenuity of man might be challenged, to show a single sentence in the constitution of the United States giving power, either direct or implied, to the general government, or any of its departments, to nullify the laws of a state, enacted for the government of its own population, or coerce obedience by force, to the mandates of the judiciary of the union. On the contrary, the journals and proceedings of the convention that framed the federal constitution, abundantly evince, that various attempts were made to effect that object, all of which were rejected. This proves that the states of this union never did, and never will permit their political rights to be suspended upon the breath of the agents or trustees, to whom they have delegated limited powers to perform certain definite acts. I, however, deem it unnecessary for me, at this time, to animadvert on this decision of the supreme court. Its fallacy, its inconsistency with former decisions, and its obvious tendency to intermeddle with the political rights of the states, and to change our federal system into one consolidated mass, has been so often exposed by the most able jurists and statesmen, that a large majority of the people of this union are confirmed in the conviction of the fallibility, infirmities and errors of this Supreme tribunal. This branch of the general Government must hence-

forth stand, where it always ought to have stood, in public estimation, as being liable to all the frailties and weakness of erring man.

Shortly after the adjournment of the legislature, in December last, I communicated directly to the president of the United States, the views of this state, as manifested by her legislature on the subject of our unoccupied lands lying in Cherokee country; and at the same time frankly communicated to him my views, as to the necessity and importance of an immediate survey, and perhaps, occupancy of these lands.

The President has manifested equal solicitude with ourselves, to effect an amicable and satisfactory adjustment of our territorial embarrassments. He has proposed to the Cherokee people, terms of the most liberal character, with a view to induce them to emigrate to the west, and thereby to enable him to effect the great object of his solicitude, in permanently benefiting that unfortunate and deluded race; and, at the same time, to fulfil the long, and delayed obligations of the United States' government to Georgia, entered into by the compact of 1802. Notwithstanding the extraordinary liberality of the proposition submitted to the Cherokees, and the kind spirit in which they were presented, the enemies of the president, and of Georgia, have so far succeeded, as to prevent any satisfactory arrangement or treaty with them; and their reply to those liberal propositions evinces a most arrogant and uncompromising spirit.

Every day's experience has afforded new evidence of the utter impracticability, and impolicy, of attempting any longer, to maintain our laws and government over the Cherokee part of Georgia, without an increased, and better population. Every effort has been made by the Executive, to maintain the inviolability of the laws of the state in Cherokee county; but these efforts have not been attended with the desired success. Our laws have been repeatedly violated, and for the want of that moral force which pervades counties inhabited by a more dense, enlightened, and virtuous population the transgressors have sometimes escaped merited punishment. Our scattered population of good character, who now inhabit this county, have often found themselves destitute of security from the depredations of dishonest men, and when they have sought protection from the laws of the land, they have often found those laws evaded, and perverted by combinations of such characters, aided by the advice and counsel of those, whose enlarged acquirements should have directed their influence in aid of the cause of justice, and the supremacy of the laws. Legal and pettifogging subtilties in this county, seem measurably to have triumphed over equity and a fair administration of the law.

Not only the supreme court of the United States, but the superior, and even the inferior courts of our own state, have so far aided in overturning our laws and the policy of our state government, as to declare them unconstitutional, and order the discharge of prisoners arrested and confined under their provisions. Nevertheless, amidst all these irregularities, strifes, and disorders, there is much cause for sincere gratification, that the events of the year have produced nothing more seriously injurious to the interest and character of the state.

The survey of the county of Cherokee, in conformity with, and under the provisions of the several acts of the legislature, has been completed without any serious obstacle or difficulty; and in the exercise of that discretion confided to me by law, I have not hesitated to move forward in that direct line, which I deemed best calculated to ensure a speedy settlement of the unoccupied lands in Cherokee county. Accordingly, in due time, the justices of the inferior courts of the several counties were notified, and required to execute the duties devolving on them, in regard to receiving and returning the names of persons entitled to draws in the lotteries; which having been done according to law, and the tickets having been prepared, the lottery commissioners were convened, and commenced the preparatory arrangements for the drawing, which was commenced on the 22d day of Oct. last, and is now in progress, under their superintendence.

I deem it unnecessary at this time to enter upon an enlarged vindication of the policy which has been pursued by the authorities of Georgia on this subject. Suffice it to say, that I have, daily, increased evidence that our policy has been founded in wisdom, justice, and true benevolence, and will, ere long terminate in the preservation of a remnant of these unfortunate Indians; and our state will be relieved from the libels and embarrassments of a thirty years' controversy.

Frances Trollope:

THE TYRANNICAL ARM OF
BRUTAL POWER

Frances Trollope, the mother of novelist Anthony Trollope and herself the author of some fifty novels, is best known today as the author of a caustic and widely read book entitled The Domestic Manners of the Americans *(1832). Coming to America from England, Mrs. Trollope failed in business (a shop in Cincinnati) but succeeded in travel. She saw a great deal of America and liked very little of what she saw.*

WE were at Washington at the time that the measure for chasing the last of several tribes of Indians from their forest homes, was canvassed in Congress, and finally decided upon by the *fiat* of the president. If the American character may be judged by their conduct in this matter, they are most lamentably deficient in every feeling of honour and integrity. It is among themselves, and from themselves, that I have heard the statements which represent them as treacherous and false almost beyond belief, in their intercourse with the unhappy Indians. Had I, during my residence in the United States, observed any single feature in their national character that could justify their eternal boast of liberality and the love of freedom, I might have respected them, however much my taste might have been offended by what was peculiar in their manners and customs. But it is impossible for any mind of common honesty not to be revolted by the contradictions in their principles and practice. They inveigh against the governments of Europe, because, as they say, they favour the powerful and oppress the weak. You may hear this declaimed upon in Congress, roared out in taverns, discussed in every drawing-room, satirized upon the stage, nay, even anathematized from the pulpit: listen to it, and then look at them at home; you will see them with one hand hoisting the cap of liberty, and with the other flogging their slaves. You will see them one hour lecturing their mob on the indefeasible rights of man, and the next driving from their homes the children of the soil, whom they have bound themselves to protect by the most solemn treaties.

In justice to those who approve not this treacherous policy, I will quote a paragraph from a New-York paper, which shows that there are some among them who look with detestation on the

Mrs. Frances Trollope, "The Tyrannical Arm of Brutal Power," from *Domestic Manners of the Americans* (London: Whittacker, Treacher & Co., 1832), pp. 180–181.

bold bad measure decided upon at Washington in the year 1830.

"We know of no subject, at the present moment, of more importance to the character of our country for justice and integrity than that which relates to the Indian tribes in Georgia and Alabama, and particularly the Cherokees in the former state. The act passed by Congress, just at the end of the session, co-operating with the tyrannical and iniquitous statute of Georgia, strikes a formidable blow at the reputation of the United States, in respect to their faith, pledged in almost innumerable instances, in the most solemn treaties and compacts."

There were many objects of much interest shown us at this Indian bureau; but, from the peculiar circumstances of this most unhappy and ill-used people, it was a very painful interest.

The dresses worn by the chiefs when their portraits were taken, are many of them splendid, from the embroidery of beads and other ornaments; and the room contains many specimens of their ingenuity, and even of their taste. There is a glass case in the room, wherein are arranged specimens of worked muslin and other needlework, some very excellent handwriting, and many other little productions of male and female Indians, all proving clearly that they are perfectly capable of civilization. Indeed, the circumstance which renders their expulsion from their own, their native lands, so peculiarly lamentable is, that they were yielding rapidly to the force of example; their lives were no longer those of wandering hunters, but they were becoming agriculturists, and the tyrannical arm of brutal power has not now driven them, as formerly, only from their hunting-grounds, their favourite springs, and the sacred bones of their fathers, but it has chased them from the dwellings their advancing knowledge had taught them to make comfortable; from the newly-ploughed fields of their pride; and from the crops their sweat had watered. And for what? To add some thousand acres of territory to the half-peopled wilderness which borders them.

Alexis de Tocqueville:
PRESENT AND FUTURE CONDITION OF THE INDIANS

Alexis de Tocqueville, an aristocratic but liberal Frenchman, came to America in 1831 in order, ostensibly, to study our penal institutions. Actually, he was tremendously excited by the prospects (and by the dangers) of a democratic society, and he wished to examine American society in its entirety. His book, De la Démocratie en Amérique *(1835), translated by Henry Reeve as* Democracy in America *(1838), is one of the most important books written about the United States.[1] Analyzing America as a nation without a feudal past, he saw egalitarianism and individualism as fundamental factors in American society. In the last chapter of Volume I, he turned to the future and singled out two problems for special study—the relations between the races and the difficulties inherent in a commercial society.*

CIVILIZATION is the result of a long social process, which takes place in the same spot, and is handed down from one generation to another, each one profiting by the experience of the last. Of all nations, those submit to civilization with the most difficulty who habitually live by the chase. Pastoral tribes, indeed, often change their place of abode; but they follow a regular order in their migrations, and often return to their old stations, whilst the dwelling of the hunter varies with that of the animals he pursues.

Several attempts have been made to diffuse knowledge amongst the Indians, leaving unchecked their wandering propensities, by the Jesuits in Canada, and by the Puritans in New England; but none of these endeavors have been crowned by any lasting success. Civilization began in the cabin, but soon retired to expire in the woods. The great error of these legislators of the Indians was their not understanding that, in order to succeed in civilizing a people, it is first necessary to fix them, which cannot be done without inducing them to cultivate the soil; the Indians ought in the first place to have been accustomed to agriculture. But not only are they destitute of this indispensable preliminary to civil'zation, they would even have great difficulty in acquiring it. Men who

[1] The dates refer to the publication of Volume I, a complete book in itself.

Alexis de Tocqueville, "Present & Future Condition of the Indians" from Democracy in America, Reeve-Bowen trans. (Cambridge: Sever & Francis, 1864), I, 439–456.

have once abandoned themselves to the restless and adventurous life of the hunter feel an insurmountable disgust for the constant and regular labor which tillage requires. We see this proved even in our own societies; but it is far more visible among races whose partiality for the chase is a part of their national character.

Independently of this general difficulty, there is another, which applies peculiarly to the Indians. They consider labor not merely as an evil, but as a disgrace; so that their pride contends against civilization as obstinately as their indolence.

There is no Indian so wretched as not to retain under his hut of bark a lofty idea of his personal worth; he considers the cares of industry as degrading occupations; he compares the husbandman to the ox which traces the furrow; and in each of our handicrafts, he can see only the labor of slaves. Not that he is devoid of admiration for the power and intellectual greatness of the whites; but, although the result of our efforts surprises him, he contemns the means by which we obtain it; and while he acknowledges our ascendency, he still believes in his own superiority. War and hunting are the only pursuits which appear to him worthy of a man. The Indian, in the dreary solitudes of his woods, cherishes the same ideas, the same opinions, as the noble of the Middle Ages in his castle; and he only needs to become a conqueror to complete the resemblance. Thus, however strange it may seem, it is in the forests of the New World, and not amongst the Europeans who people its coasts, that the ancient prejudices of Europe still exist.

More than once, in the course of this work, I have endeavored to explain the prodigious influence which the social condition appears to exercise upon the laws and the manners of men; and I beg to add a few words on the same subject.

When I perceive the resemblance which exists between the political institutions of our ancestors, the Germans, and the wandering tribes of North America—between the customs described by Tacitus, and those of which I have sometimes been a witness—I cannot help thinking that the same cause has brought about the same results in both hemispheres; and that, in the midst of the apparent diversity of human affairs, certain primary facts may be discovered, from which all the others are derived. In what we usually call the German institutions, then, I am inclined to perceive only barbarian habits, and the opinions of savages in what we style feudal principles.

However strongly the vices and prejudices of the North American Indians may be opposed to their becoming agricultural and civilized, necessity sometimes drives them to it. Several of the Southern tribes, considerably numerous, and amongst others the Cherokees and the Creeks,[2] found themselves, as it were, surrounded by Europeans, who had landed on the shores of the Atlantic, and, either descending the Ohio, or proceeding up the Mississippi, arrived simultaneously upon their borders. These tribes had not been driven from place to place, like their Northern brethren; but

[2] These nations are now swallowed up in the States of Georgia, Tennessee, Alabama, and Mississippi. There were formerly in the South four great nations (remnants of which still exist), the Choctaws, the Chickasaws, the Creeks, and the Cherokees. The remnants of these four nations amounted in 1830 to about 75,000 individuals. It is computed that there are now remaining in the territory occupied or claimed by the Anglo-American Union about 300,000 Indians.

they had been gradually shut up within narrow limits, like game driven into an enclosure before the huntsmen plunge among them. The Indians, who were thus placed between civilization and death, found themselves obliged to live ignominiously by labor, like the whites. They took to agriculture, and, without entirely forsaking their old habits or manners, sacrificed only as much as was necessary to their existence.

The Cherokees went further; they created a written language, established a permanent form of government, and, as everything proceeds rapidly in the New World, before they all of them had clothes, they set up a newspaper.

The development of European habits has been much accelerated among these Indians by the mixed race which has sprung up. Deriving intelligence from the father's side, without entirely losing the savage customs of the mother, the half-blood forms the natural link between civilization and barbarism. Wherever this race has multiplied, the savage state has become modified, and a great change has taken place in the manners of the people.[3]

The success of the Cherokees proves that the Indians are capable of civilization, but it does not prove that they will succeed in it. This difficulty which the Indians find in submitting to civilization proceeds from a general cause, the influence of which it is almost impossible for them to escape. An attentive survey of history demonstrates that, in general, barbarous nations have raised themselves to civilization by degrees, and by their own efforts. Whenever they derived knowledge from a foreign people, they stood towards them in the relation of conquerors, and not of a conquered nation. When the conquered nation is enlightened, and the conquerors are half savage, as in the invasion of the Roman empire by the Northern nations, or that of China by the Mongols, the power which victory bestows upon the barbarian is sufficient to keep up his importance among civilized men, and permit him to rank as their equal until he becomes their rival. The one has might on his side, the other has intelligence; the former admires the knowledge and the arts of the conquered, the latter envies the power of the conquerors. The barbarians at length admit civilized man into their palaces, and he in turn opens his schools to the barbarians. But when the side on which the physical force lies also possesses an intellectual superiority, the conquered party seldom becomes

[3] Unhappily, the mixed race has been less numerous and less influential in North America than in any other country. The American continent was peopled by two great nations of Europe, the French and the English. The former were not slow in connecting themselves with the daughters of the natives; but there was an unfortunate affinity between the Indian character and their own: instead of giving the tastes and habits of civilized life to the savages, the French too often grew passionately fond of Indian life. They became the most dangerous inhabitants of the desert, and won the friendship of the Indian by exaggerating his vices and his virtues. M. de Senonville, the Governor of Canada, wrote thus to Louis XIV in 1685: "It has long been believed that, in order to civilize the savages, we ought to draw them nearer to us. But there is every reason to suppose we have been mistaken. Those which have been brought into contact with us have not become French, and the French who have lived among them are changed into savages, affecting to dress and live like them." (*History of New France*, by Charlevoix, Vol. II, p. 345.) The Englishman, on the contrary, continuing obstinately attached to the customs and the most insignificant habits of his forefathers, has remained in the midst of the American solitudes just what he was in the bosom of European cities; he would not allow of any communication with savages whom he despised, and avoided with care the union of his race with theirs. Thus, while the French exercised no salutary influence over the Indians, the English have always remained alien from them.

88

civilized; it retreats, or is destroyed. It may therefore be said, in a general way, that savages go forth in arms to seek knowledge, but do not receive it when it comes to them.

If the Indian tribes which now inhabit the heart of the continent could summon up energy enough to attempt to civilize themselves, they might possibly succeed. Superior already to the barbarous nations which surround them, they would gradually gain strength and experience, and when the Europeans should appear upon their borders, they would be in a state, if not to maintain their independence, at least to assert their right to the soil, and to incorporate themselves with the conquerors. But it is the misfortune of Indians to be brought into contact with a civilized people, who are also (it must be owned) the most grasping nation on the globe, whilst they are still semi-barbarian; to find their masters in their instructors, and to receive knowledge and oppression at once. Living in the freedom of the woods, the North American Indian was destitute, but he had no feeling of inferiority towards any one; as soon, however, as he desires to penetrate into the social scale of the whites, he can only take the lowest rank in society, for he enters, ignorant and poor, within the pale of science and wealth. After having led a life of agitation, beset with evils and dangers, but at the same time filled with proud emotions, he is obliged to submit to a wearisome, obscure, and degraded state. To gain the bread which nourishes him by hard and ignoble labor—this is in his eyes the only result of which civilization can boast; and even this he is not always sure to obtain.

When the Indians undertake to imitate their European neighbors, and to till the earth like them, they are immediately exposed to a formidable competition. The white man is skilled in the craft of agriculture; the Indian is a rough beginner in an art with which he is unacquainted. The former reaps abundant crops without difficulty, the latter meets with a thousand obstacles in raising the fruits of the earth.

The European is placed amongst a population whose wants he knows and partakes. The savage is isolated in the midst of a hostile people, with whose manners, language, and laws he is imperfectly acquainted, but without whose assistance he cannot live. He can only procure the materials of comfort by bartering his commodities for the goods of the European, for the assistance of his countrymen is wholly insufficient to supply his wants. Thus, when the Indian wishes to sell the produce of his labor, he cannot always find a purchaser, whilst the European readily obtains a market; the former can only produce at considerable cost what the latter sells at a low rate. Thus the Indian has no sooner escaped those evils to which barbarous nations are exposed, than he is subjected to the still greater miseries of civilized communities; and he finds it scarcely less difficult to live in the midst of our abundance, than in the depth of his own forest.

He has not yet lost the habits of his erratic life; the traditions of his fathers and his passion for the chase are still alive within him. The wild enjoyments which formerly animated him in the woods painfully excite his troubled imagination; the privations which he endured there appear less keen, his former perils less appalling. He contrasts the independence which he possessed amongst his equals with the servile position which he occupies in civilized society. On the other hand, the solitudes which were so long his free home are still at hand; a few hours' march will bring him back to them once more. The whites offer him a sum, which seems to him considerable, for the half-cleared ground whence he obtains sustenance with difficulty. This money of the Europeans may possibly enable him to live a happy and tranquil life far away from them; and he quits the plough, resumes his native arms, and returns to the wilderness forever. The condition of the Creeks and Cherokees, to which I have already alluded, sufficiently corroborates the truth of this sad picture.

The Indians, in the little which they have done, have unquestionably displayed as much natural genius as the peoples of Europe in their greatest undertakings; but nations as well as men require time to learn, whatever may be their intelligence and their zeal. Whilst the savages were endeavoring to civilize themselves, the Europeans continued to surround them on every side, and to confine them within narrower limits; the two races gradually met, and they are now in immediate contact with each other. The Indian is already superior to his barbarous parent, but he is still far below his white neighbor. With their resources and acquired knowledge, the Europeans soon appropriated to themselves most of the advantages which the natives might have derived from the possession of the soil: they have settled among them, have purchased land at a low rate, or have occupied it by force, and the Indians have been ruined by a competition which they had not the means of sustaining. They were isolated in their own country, and their race only constituted a little colony of troublesome strangers in the midst of a numerous and dominant people.[4]

Washington said, in one of his messages to Congress, "We are more enlightened and more powerful than the Indian nations; we are therefore bound in honor to treat them with kindness, and even with generosity." But this virtuous and high-minded policy has not been followed. The rapacity of the settlers is usually backed by the tyranny of the government. Although the Cherokees and the Creeks are established upon territory which they inhabited before the arrival of the Europeans, and although the Americans have frequently treated with them as with foreign nations, the surrounding States have not been willing to acknowledge them as an independent people, and have undertaken to subject these children of the woods to Anglo-American magistrates, laws, and customs. Destitution had driven these unfortunate Indians to civilization, and oppression now drives them back to barbarism: many of them abandon the soil which they had begun

[4] See in the Legislative Documents (21st Congress, No. 89) instances of excesses of every kind committed by the whites upon the territory of the Indians, either in taking possession of a part of their lands, until compelled to retire by the troops of Congress, or carrying off their cattle, burning their houses, cutting down their corn, and doing violence to their persons.

The Union has a representative agent continually employed to reside among the Indians; and the report of the Cherokee agent, which is among the documents I have referred to, is almost always favorable to the Indians. "The intrusion of whites," he says, "upon the lands of the Cherokees will cause ruin to the poor, helpless, and inoffensive inhabitants." And he further remarks upon the attempt of the State of Georgia to establish a boundary line for the country of the Cherokees, that the line, having been made by the whites alone, and entirely upon *ex parte* evidence of their several rights, was of no validity whatever.

to clear, and return to the habits of savage life.

If we consider the tyrannical measures which have been adopted by the legislatures of the Southern States, the conduct of their Governors, and the decrees of their courts of justice, we shall be convinced that the entire expulsion of the Indians is the final result to which all the efforts of their policy are directed. The Americans of that part of the Union look with jealousy upon the lands which the natives still possess;[5] they are aware that these tribes have not yet lost the traditions of savage life, and before civilization has permanently fixed them to the soil, it is intended to force them to depart by reducing them to despair. The Creeks and Cherokees, oppressed by the several States, have appealed to the central government, which is by no means insensible to their misfortunes, and is sincerely desirous of saving the remnant of the natives, and of maintaining them in the free possession of that territory which the Union has guaranteed to them. But the several States oppose so formidable a resistance to the execution of this design, that the government is obliged to consent to the extirpation of a few barbarous tribes, already half destroyed, in order not to endanger the safety of the American Union.

But the Federal government, which is not able to protect the Indians, would fain mitigate the hardships of their lot; and, with this intention, it has undertaken to transport them into remote regions at the public cost.

Between the 33d and 37th degrees of north latitude, a vast tract of country

[5] The Georgians, who are so much troubled by the proximity of the Indians, inhabit a territory which does not at present contain more than seven inhabitants to the square mile. In France, there are one hundred and sixty-two inhabitants to the same extent of country.

lies, which has taken the name of Arkansas, from the principal river that waters it. It is bounded on the one side by the confines of Mexico, on the other by the Mississippi. Numberless streams cross it in every direction; the climate is mild, and the soil productive, and it is inhabited only by a few wandering hordes of savages. The government of the Union wishes to transport the broken remnants of the indigenous population of the South to the portion of this country which is nearest to Mexico, and at a great distance from the American settlements.

We were assured, towards the end of the year 1831, that 10,000 Indians had already gone to the shores of the Arkansas, and fresh detachments were constantly following them. But Congress has been unable to create a unanimous determination in those whom it is disposed to protect. Some, indeed, joyfully consent to quit the seat of oppression; but the most enlightened members of the community refuse to abandon their recent dwellings and their springing crops; they are of the opinion that the work of civilization, once interrupted, will never be resumed; they fear that those domestic habits which have been so recently contracted may be irrevocably lost in the midst of a country which is still barbarous, and where nothing is prepared for the subsistence of an agricultural people; they know that their entrance into those wilds will be opposed by hostile hordes, and that they have lost the energy of barbarians, without having yet acquired the resources of civilization to resist their attacks. Moreover, the Indians readily discover that the settlement which is proposed to them is merely temporary. Who can assure them that they will at length be allowed to dwell in peace in their new retreat? The United States pledge themselves to maintain them there; but the territory which they now occupy was formerly secured to them by the most solemn oaths.[6] The American government does not indeed now rob them of their lands, but it allows perpetual encroachments on them. In a few years, the same white population which now flocks around them will doubtless track them anew to the solitudes of the Arkansas; they will then be exposed to the same evils, without the same remedies; and as the limits of the earth will at last fail them, their only refuge is the grave.

The Union treats the Indians with less cupidity and violence than the several States, but the two governments are alike deficient in good faith. The States extend what they call the benefits of their laws to the Indians, believing that the tribes will recede rather than submit to them; and the central government, which promises a permanent refuge to these unhappy beings in the West, is well aware of its inability to secure it to them.[7] Thus the tyranny of the States

obliges the savages to retire; the Union, by its promises and resources, facilitates their retreat; and these measures tend to precisely the same end.

"By the will of our Father in Heaven, the Governor of the whole world," said the Cherokees, in their petition to Congress,[8] "the red man of America has become small, and the white man great and renowned. When the ancestors of the people of these United States first came to the shores of America, they found the red man strong: though he was ignorant and savage, yet he received them kindly, and gave them dry land to rest their weary feet. They met in peace, and shook hands in token of friendship. Whatever the white man wanted and asked of the Indian, the latter willingly gave. At that time, the Indian was the lord, and the white man the suppliant. But now the scene has changed. The strength of the red man has become weakness. As his neighbors increased in numbers, his power became less and less; and now, of the many and powerful tribes who once covered these United States, only a few are to be seen, —a few whom a sweeping pestilence has left. The Northern tribes, who were once so numerous and powerful, are now nearly extinct. Thus it has happened to the red man of America. Shall we, who are remnants, share the same fate?

"The land on which we stand we have

[6] The fifth article of the treaty made with the Creeks in August, 1790, is in the following words: "The United States solemnly guarantee to the Creek nation all their land within the limits of the United States." The seventh article of the treaty concluded in 1791 with the Cherokees says: "The United States solemnly guarantee to the Cherokee nation all their lands not hereby ceded." The following article declared that, if any citizen of the United States, or other settler not of the Indian race, should establish himself upon the territory of the Cherokees, the United States would withdraw their protection from that individual, and give him up to be punished as the Cherokee nation should think fit.

[7] This does not prevent them from promising in the most solemn manner to do so. See the letter of the President addressed to the Creek Indians, 23d March, 1829. "Beyond the great river Mississippi, where a part of your nation has gone, your father has provided a country large enough for all of you, and he advises you to remove to it. There your white brothers will not trouble you; they will have no claim to the land, and you can live upon it, you and all your

children, as long as the grass grows, or the water runs, in peace and plenty. *It will be yours forever.*"

The Secretary of War, in a letter written to the Cherokees, April 18th, 1829, declares to them that they cannot expect to retain possession of the lands at that time occupied by them, but gives them the most positive assurance of uninterrupted peace if they would remove beyond the Mississippi: as if the power which could not grant them protection then, would be able to afford it them hereafter!

[8] December 18th, 1829.

received as an inheritance from our fathers, who possessed it from time immemorial, as a gift from our common Father in Heaven. They bequeathed it to us as their children, and we have sacredly kept it, as containing the remains of our beloved men. This right of inheritance we have never ceded, nor ever forfeited. Permit us to ask, what better right can the people have to a country than the right of inheritance and immemorial peaceable possession? We know it is said of late by the State of Georgia and by the Executive of the United States, that we have forfeited this right; but we think this is said gratuitously. At what time have we made the forfeit? What great crime have we committed, whereby we must forever be divested of our country and rights? Was it when we were hostile to the United States, and took part with the king of Great Britain, during the struggle for independence? If so, why was not this forfeiture declared in the first treaty of peace between the United States and our beloved men? Why was not such an article as the following inserted in the treaty: 'The United States give peace to the Cherokees, but, for the part they took in the late war, declare them to be but tenants at will, to be removed when the convenience of the States within whose chartered limits they live shall require it'? That was the proper time to assume such a position. But it was not thought of; nor would our forefathers have agreed to any treaty whose tendency was to deprive them of their rights and their country."

Such is the language of the Indians: what they say is true; what they foresee seems inevitable. From whichever side we consider the destinies of the aborigines of North America, their calamities appear irremediable: if they continue barbarous, they are forced to retire; if they attempt to civilize themselves, the contact of a more civilized community subjects them to oppression and destitution. They perish if they continue to wander from waste to waste, and if they attempt to settle, they still must perish. The assistance of Europeans is necessary to instruct them, but the approach of Europeans corrupts and repels them into savage life. They refuse to change their habits as long as their solitudes are their own, and it is too late to change them when at last they are constrained to submit.

The Spaniards pursued the Indians with blood-hounds, like wild beasts; they sacked the New World like a city taken by storm, with no discernment or compassion; but destruction must cease at last, and frenzy has a limit: the remnant of the Indian population which had escaped the massacre mixed with its conquerors, and adopted in the end their religion and their manners.[9] The conduct of the Americans of the United States towards the aborigines is characterized, on the other hand, by a singular attachment to the formalities of law. Provided that the Indians retain their barbarous condition, the Americans take no part in their affairs; they treat them as independent nations, and do not possess themselves of their hunting-grounds without a treaty of purchase; and if an Indian nation happen to be so encroached upon as to be unable to subsist upon their territory, they kindly take them by the hand and transport them to a grave far from the land of their fathers.

[9] The honor of this result is, however, by no means due to the Spaniards. If the Indian tribes had not been tillers of the ground at the time of the arrival of the Europeans, they would unquestionably have been destroyed in South as well as in North America.

The Spaniards were unable to exterminate the Indian race by those unparalleled atrocities which brand them with indelible shame, nor did they even succeed in wholly depriving it of its rights; but the Americans of the United States have accomplished this twofold purpose with singular felicity, tranquilly, legally, philanthropically, without shedding blood, and without violating a single great principle of morality in the eyes of the world.[10] It is impossible to destroy men with more respect for the laws of humanity.

[10] See, amongst other documents, the Report made by Mr. Bell in the name of the Committee on Indian Affairs, Feb. 24th, 1830, in which it is most logically established, and most learnedly proved, that "the fundamental principle, that the Indians had no right, by virtue of their ancient possession, either of soil or sovereignty, has never been abandoned either expressly or by implication."

In perusing this Report, which is evidently drawn up by a skillful hand, one is astonished at the facility with which the author gets rid of all arguments founded upon reason and natural right, which he designates as abstract and theoretical principles. The more I contemplate the difference between civilized and uncivilized man with regard to the principles of justice, the more I observe that the former contests the foundation of those rights, which the latter simply violates. [Mr. Bell, of Tennessee, was chairman of the Committee on which Wilson Lumpkin served. [ED.'s NOTE]

Ralph Waldo Emerson:

LETTER TO MARTIN VAN BUREN

In 1836, just as Andrew Jackson's administration was coming to an end, an unknown New Englander published a short book entitled Nature. *It was a revolutionary book, the most important theoretical document of the Transcendentalist movement. If any American other than Andrew Jackson can be taken as the eponym of his age, that American is surely Ralph Waldo Emerson; and yet, in writing to President Van Buren, Emerson was, in a sense, turning away from his major theme: a reliance on the Self. The letter was one of Emerson's rare sorties into political life, and, as such, it is all the more interesting.*

SIR: The seat you fill places you in a relation of credit and nearness to every citizen. By right and natural position, every citizen is your friend. Before any acts contrary to his own judgment or interest have repelled the affections of any man, each may look with trust and living anticipation to your government. Each has the highest right to call your attention to such subjects as are of a public nature, and properly belong to the chief magistrate; and the good magistrate will feel a joy in meeting such confidence. In this belief and at the instance of a few of my friends and neighbors, I crave of your patience a short hearing for their sentiments and my own: and the circumstance that my name will be utterly unknown to you will only give the fairer chance to your equitable construction of what I have to say.

Sir, my communication respects the sinister rumors that fill this part of the country concerning the Cherokee people. The interest always felt in the aboriginal population—an interest naturally growing as that decays—has been heightened in regard to this tribe. Even in our distant State some good rumor of their worth and civility has arrived. We have learned with joy their improvement in the social arts. We have read their newspapers. We have seen some of them in our schools and colleges. In common with the great body of the American people, we have witnessed with sympathy the painful labors of these red men to redeem their own race from the doom of eternal inferiority, and to borrow and domesticate in the tribe the arts and customs of the Caucasian race. And notwithstanding the unaccountable apathy with which of late years the Indians have been sometimes abandoned to their enemies, it is not to be doubted that it is the good pleasure and the

Ralph Waldo Emerson, "Letter to President Van Buren," *Complete Works* (Centenary Ed.), (Boston: Houghton Mifflin, 1903–04), XI, 89–96.

understanding of all humane persons in the Republic, of the men and the matrons sitting in the thriving independent families all over the land, that they shall be duly cared for; that they shall taste justice and love from all to whom we have delegated the office of dealing with them.

The newspapers now inform us that, in December, 1835, a treaty contracting for the exchange of all the Cherokee territory was pretended to be made by an agent on the part of the United States with some persons appearing on the part of the Cherokees; that the fact afterwards transpired that these deputies did by no means represent the will of the nation; and that, out of eighteen thousand souls composing the nation, fifteen thousand six hundred and sixty-eight have protested against the so-called treaty. It now appears that the government of the United States choose to hold the Cherokees to this sham treaty, and are proceeding to execute the same. Almost the entire Cherokee Nation stand up and say, "This is not our act. Behold us. Here are we. Do not mistake that handful of deserters for us"; and the American President and the Cabinet, the Senate and the House of Representatives, neither hear these men nor see them, and are contracting to put this active nation into carts and boats, and to drag them over mountains and rivers to a wilderness at a vast distance beyond the Mississippi. And a paper purporting to be an army order fixes a month from this day as the hour for this doleful removal.

In the name of God, sir, we ask you if this be so. Do the newspapers rightly inform us? Men and women with pale and perplexed faces meet one another in the streets and churches here, and ask if this be so. We have inquired if this

be a gross misrepresentation from the party opposed to the government and anxious to blacken it with the people. We have looked at the newspapers of different parties and find a horrid confirmation of the tale. We are slow to believe it. We hoped the Indians were misinformed, and that their remonstrance was premature, and will turn out to be a needless act of terror.

The piety, the principle that is left in the United States, if only in its coarsest form, a regard to the speech of men, forbid us to entertain it as a fact. Such a dereliction of all faith and virtue, such a denial of justice, and such deafness to screams for mercy were never heard of in times of peace and in the dealing of a nation with its own allies and wards, since the earth was made. Sir, does this government think that the people of the United States are become savage and mad? From their mind are the sentiments of love and a good nature wiped clean out? The soul of man, the justice, the mercy that is the heart's heart in all men, from Maine to Georgia, does abhor this business.

In speaking thus the sentiments of my neighbors and my own, perhaps I overstep the bounds of decorum. But would it not be a higher indecorum coldly to argue a matter like this? We only state the fact that a crime is projected that confounds our understandings by its magnitude, a crime that really deprives us as well as the Cherokees of a country for how could we call the conspiracy that should crush these poor Indians our government, or the land that was cursed by their parting and dying imprecations our country, any more? You, sir, will bring down that renowned chair in which you sit into infamy if your seal is set to this instrument of perfidy; and the name of this nation, hitherto the sweet omen of religion and liberty, will stink to the world.

You will not do us the injustice of connecting this remonstrance with any sectional and party feeling. It is in our hearts the simplest commandment of brotherly love. We will not have this great and solemn claim upon national and human justice huddled aside under the flimsy plea of its being a party act. Sir, to us the questions upon which the government and the people have been agitated during the past year, touching the prostration of the currency and of trade, seem but motes in comparison. These hard times, it is true, have brought the discussion home to every farmhouse and poor man's house in this town; but it is the chirping of grasshoppers beside the immortal question whether justice shall be done by the race of civilized to the race of savage man, whether all the attributes of reason, of civility, of justice, and even of mercy, shall be put off by the American people, and so vast an outrage upon the Cherokee Nation and upon human nature shall be consummated.

One circumstance lessens the reluctance with which I intrude at this time on your attention my conviction that the government ought to be admonished of a new historical fact, which the discussion of this question has disclosed, namely, that there exists in a great part of the Northern people a gloomy diffidence in the *moral* character of the government.

On the broaching of this question, a general expression of despondency, of disbelief that any good will accrue from a remonstrance on an act of fraud and robbery, appeared in those men to whom we naturally turn for aid and counsel. Will the American government steal?

Will it lie? Will it kill?—We ask triumphantly. Our counsellors and old statesmen here say that ten years ago they would have staked their lives on the affirmation that the proposed Indian measures could not be executed; that the unanimous country would put them down. And now the steps of this crime follow each other so fast, at such fatally quick time, that the millions of virtuous citizens, whose agents the government are, have no place to interpose, and must shut their eyes until the last howl and wailing of these tormented villages and tribes shall afflict the ear of the world.

I will not hide from you, as an indication of the alarming distrust, that a letter addressed as mine is, and suggesting to the mind of the Executive the plain obligations of man, has a burlesque character in the apprehensions of some of my friends. I, sir, will not beforehand treat you with the contumely of this distrust. I will at least state to you this fact, and show you how plain and humane people, whose love would be honor, regard the policy of the government, and what injurious inferences they draw as to the minds of the governors. A man with your experience in affairs must have seen cause to appreciate the futility of opposition to the moral sentiment. However feeble the sufferer and however great the oppressor, it is in the nature of things that the blow should recoil upon the aggressor. For God is in the sentiment, and it cannot be withstood. The potentate and the people perish before it; but with it, and its executor, they are omnipotent.

I write thus, sir, to inform you of the state of mind these Indian tidings have awakened here, and to pray with one voice more that you, whose hands are strong with the delegated power of fif-

teen millions of men, will avert with
that might the terrific injury which
threatens the Cherokee tribe.

With great respect, sir, I am your
fellow citizen,

RALPH WALDO EMERSON.

Helen Hunt Jackson:

GEORGIA'S DISHONOR

Helen Hunt Jackson, of Amherst, Massachusetts, is known chiefly for two books, both of which deal with the problem of the American Indian. Ramona, a novel published in 1884, dramatizes the plight of the Indians in California. A Century of Dishonor, published in 1881, remains the best known of the innumerable indictments of state and federal Indian policy.

IN the whole history of our Government's dealings with the Indian tribes, there is no record so black as the record of its perfidy to this nation. There will come a time in the remote future when, to the student of American history, it will seem well-nigh incredible. From the beginning of the century they had been steadily advancing in civilization. As far back as 1800 they had begun the manufacture of cotton cloth, and in 1820 there was scarcely a family in that part of the nation living east of the Mississippi but what understood the use of the card and spinning-wheel. Every family had its farm under cultivation. The territory was laid off into districts, with a council-house, a judge, and a marshal in each district. A national committee and council were the supreme authority in the nation. Schools were flourishing in all the villages. Printing-presses were at work.

Their territory was larger than the three States of Massachusetts, Rhode Island, and Connecticut combined. It embraced the North-western part of Georgia, the North-east of Alabama, a corner of Tennessee and of North Carolina. They were enthusiastic in their efforts to establish and perfect their own system of jurisprudence. Missions of several sects were established in their country, and a large number of them had professed Christianity, and were living exemplary lives.

There is no instance in all history of a race of people passing in so short a space of time from the barbarous stage to the agricultural and civilized. And it was such a community as this that the State of Georgia, by one high-handed outrage, made outlaws!—passing on the 19th of December, 1829, a law "to annul all laws and ordinances made by the Cherokee nation of Indians"; declaring "all laws, ordinances, orders, and regulations of any kind whatever, made, passed, or enacted by the Cherokee Indians, either in general council or in any other way whatever, or by any authority whatever, null and void, and of

Helen Hunt Jackson, "Georgia's Dishonor," from *A Century of Dishonor* (New York: Harper and Brothers, 1881), pp. 270–279.

no effect, as if the same had never existed; also, that no Indian, or descendant of any Indian residing within the Creek or Cherokee nations of Indians, shall be deemed a competent witness in any court of this State to which a white man may be a party."

What had so changed the attitude of Georgia to the Indians within her borders? Simply the fact that the Indians, finding themselves hemmed in on all sides by fast thickening white settlements, had taken a firm stand that they would give up no more land. So long as they would cede and cede, and grant and grant tract after tract, and had millions of acres still left to cede and grant, the selfishness of white men took no alarm; but once consolidated into an empire, with fixed and inalienable boundaries, powerful, recognized, and determined, the Cherokee nation would be a thorn in the flesh to her white neighbors. The doom of the Cherokees was sealed on the day when they declared, once for all, officially as a nation, that they would not sell another foot of land. This they did in an interesting and pathetic message to the United States Senate in 1822.

Georgia, through her governor and her delegates to Congress, had been persistently demanding to have the Cherokees compelled to give up their lands. She insisted that the United States Government should fulfil a provision, made in an old compact of 1802, to extinguish the Indian titles within her limits as soon as it could be peaceably done. This she demanded should be done now, either peaceably or otherwise.

"We cannot but view the design of those letters," says this message, "as an attempt bordering on a hostile disposition toward the Cherokee nation to wrest from them by arbitrary means their just rights and liberties, the security of which is solemnly guaranteed to them by these United States. . . . We assert under the fullest authority that all the sentiments expressed in relation to the disposition and determination of the nation never to cede another foot of land, are positively the production and voice of the nation. . . . There is not a spot out of the limits of any of the States or Territories thereof, and within the limits of the United States, that they would ever consent to inhabit; because they have unequivocally determined never again to pursue the chase as heretofore, or to engage in wars, unless by the common call of the Government to defend the common rights of the United States. . . . The Cherokees have turned their attention to the pursuits of the civilized man: agriculture, manufactures, and the mechanic arts and education are all in successful operation in the nation at this time; and while the Cherokees are peacefully endeavoring to enjoy the blessings of civilization and Christianity on the soil of their rightful inheritance, and while the exertions and labors of various religious societies of these United States are successfully engaged in promulgating to them the words of truth and life from the sacred volume of Holy Writ, and under the patronage of the General Government, they are threatened with removal or extinction. . . . We appeal to the magnanimity of the American Congress for justice, and the protection of the rights and liberties and lives of the Cherokee people. We claim it from the United States by the strongest obligation which imposes it on them—by treaties: and we expect it from them under that memorable declaration, 'that all men are created equal; that they are endowed by their Creator with certain inalienable rights; that among these are life, liberty, and the pursuit of happiness.' "

The dignified and pathetic remonstrances of the Cherokee chiefs, their firm reiterations of their resolve not to part with their lands, were called by the angry Georgian governor "tricks of vulgar cunning," and "insults from the polluted lips of outcasts and vagabonds"; and he is not afraid, in an official letter to the Secretary of War, to openly threaten the President that, if he upholds the Indians in their rejection of the overtures for removal, the "consequences are inevitable," and that, in resisting the occupation of the Cherokee lands by the Georgians, he will be obliged to "make war upon, and shed the blood of brothers and friends."

. . . Never did mountaineers cling more desperately to their homes than did the Cherokees. The State of Georgia put the whole nation in duress, but still they chose to stay. Year by year high-handed oppressions increased and multiplied; military law reigned everywhere; Cherokee lands were surveyed, and put up to be drawn by lottery; missionaries were arrested and sent to prison for preaching to Cherokees; Cherokees were sentenced to death by Georgia juries, and hung by Georgia executioners. Appeal after appeal to the President and to Congress for protection produced only reiterated confessions of the Government's inability to protect them— reiterated proposals to them to accept a price for their country and move away. Nevertheless they clung to it. A few hundreds went, but the body of the nation still protested and entreated. There is nothing in history more touching than the cries of this people to the Government of the United States to fulfil its promises to them. And their cause

was not without eloquent advocates. When the bill for their removal was before Congress, Frelinghuysen, Sprague, Robbins, Storrs, Ellsworth, Evans, Huntington, Johns, Bates, Crockett, Everett, Test—all spoke warmly against it; and, to the credit of Congress be it said, the bill passed the Senate by only one majority.

The Rev. Jeremiah Evarts published a series of papers in the *National Intelligencer* under the signature of William Penn, in which he gave a masterly analysis and summing up of the case, recapitulated the sixteen treaties which the Government had made with the Cherokees, all guaranteeing to them their lands, and declared that the Government had "arrived at the bank of the Rubicon," where it must decide if it would or would not save the country from the charge of bad faith. Many of his eloquent sentences read in the light of the present time like prophecies. He says, "in a quarter of a century the pressure upon the Indians will be much greater from the boundless prairies, which must ultimately be subdued and inhabited, than it would ever have been from the borders of the present Cherokee country"; and asks, pertinently, "to what confidence would such an engagement be entitled, done at the very moment that treaties with Indians are declared not to be binding, and for the very reason that existing treaties are not strong enough to bind the United States." Remonstrances poured in upon Congress, petitions and memorials from religious societies, from little country villages, all imploring the Government to keep its faith to these people.

The Cherokees' own newspaper, *The Phoenix*, was filled at this time with the records of the nation's suffering and despair.

"The State of Georgia has taken a strong stand against us, and the United States must either defend us and our rights or leave us to our foe. In the latter case she will violate her promise of protection, and we cannot in future depend upon any guarantee to us, either here or beyond the Mississippi.

"If the United States shall withdraw their solemn pledges of protection, utterly disregard their plighted faith, deprive us of the right of self-government, and wrest from us our land, then, in the deep anguish of our misfortunes, we may justly say there is no place of security for us, no confidence left that the United States will be more just and faithful toward us in the barren prairies of the West than when we occupied the soil inherited from the Great Author of our existence."

As a last resort the Cherokees carried their case before the Supreme Court, and implored that body to restrain the State of Georgia from her unjust interference with their rights. The reports of the case of the Cherokee Nation vs. the State of Georgia fill a volume by themselves, and are of vital importance to the history of Indian affairs. The majority of the judges decided that an Indian tribe could not be considered as a foreign nation, and therefore could not bring the suit. Judge Thompson and Judge Story dissented from this opinion, and held that the Cherokee tribe did constitute a foreign nation, and that the State of Georgia ought to be enjoined from execution of its unjust laws. The opinion of Chancellor Kent coincided with that of Judges Thompson and Story. Chancellor Kent gave it as his opinion that the cases in which the Supreme Court had jurisdiction would "reach and embrace every controversy that can arise between the Cherokees and the State of Georgia or its officers under the execution of the act of Georgia."

But all this did not help the Cherokees; neither did the fact of the manifest sympathy of the whole court with their wrongs. The technical legal decision had been rendered against them, and this delivered them over to the tender mercies of Georgia: no power in the land could help them. Fierce factions now began to be formed in the nation, one for and one against the surrender of their lands. Many were ready still to remain and suffer till death rather than give them up; but wiser counsels prevailed, and in the last days of the year 1835 a treaty was concluded with the United States by twenty of the Cherokee chiefs and headmen, who thereby, in behalf of their nation, relinquished all the lands claimed or possessed by them east of the Mississippi River.

Frederick Jackson Turner:

THE ADVANCE OF THE
GEORGIA FRONTIER

Meeting in Chicago to help celebrate the Columbian Exposition of 1893, the American Historical Association heard a young scholar read a short paper that was to become one of the most influential essays ever written by an American historian. Frederick Jackson Turner's essay, "The Significance of the Frontier in American History," has had a widespread and an enduring influence on American historiography. Few scholars today would attempt to write of the development of American civilization without taking into account the significance of the frontier. Nevertheless, Turner's hypothesis had serious difficulties, and Turner, in attempting to reconcile his theory of frontier democracy with the frontier's tendency to repudiate the institutions of society, shows an awareness of some of these difficulties.

FROM the beginning of the nation, the Indians on the borders of the settled area of Georgia were a menace and an obstacle to her development. Indeed, they constituted a danger to the United States as well: their pretensions to independence and complete sovereignty over their territory were at various times utilized by adventurers from France, England, and Spain as a means of promoting the designs of these powers. Jackson drove a wedge between the Indian confederacies of this region by his victories in the War of 1812 and the cessions which followed. Although, in 1821, a large belt of territory between the Ocmulgee and Flint rivers was ceded by the Creeks to Georgia, the state saw with impatience some of the best lands still occupied by these Indians in the territory lying between the Flint and the Chattahoochee.

The spectacle of a stream of Georgia settlers crossing this rich Indian area of their own state to settle in the lands newly acquired in Alabama and Mississippi provoked Georgia's wrath, and numerous urgent calls were made upon the government to carry out the agreement made in 1802, by completing the acquisition of these Indian lands. Responding to this demand, a treaty was made at Indian Springs in February, 1825, by which the Creeks ceded all of

From Frederick Jackson Turner, *The Rise of the New West.* Copyright 1906 by Harper & Brothers, pp. 309–313, and Frederick Jackson Turner, *The United States: 1830–1850* (New York: Henry Holt & Co., 1935), pp. 393–394. Reprinted by permission of the publishers.

their lands in Georgia; but when Adams came to the presidency he was confronted with a serious situation arising from this treaty. Shortly after it had been ratified, McIntosh, a principal chief of the Lower Creeks, who had signed the treaty, contrary to the rule of the tribe and in spite of the decision to sell no more land, was put to death; and the whole treaty was repudiated by the great body of the Creeks, as having been procured by fraud and made by a small minority of their nation. The difficulty arose from the fact that the various villages of these Indians were divided into opposing parties: the Upper Creeks, living chiefly along the forks of the Alabama, on the Tallapoosa and the Coosa in Alabama, constituting the more numerous branch, were determined to yield no more territory, while the principal chiefs of the Lower Creeks, who dwelt in western Georgia, along the Flint and Chattahoochee branches of the Apalachicola, were not unfavorable to removal.

When Governor Troup, of Georgia, determined to survey the ceded lands, he was notified that the president expected Georgia to abandon the survey until it could be done consistently with the provisions of the treaty. Although the treaty had given the Creeks until September, 1826, to vacate, Governor Troup informed General Gaines, who had been sent to preserve peace, that, as there existed "two independent parties to the question, each is permitted to decide for itself," and he announced that the line would be run and the survey effected. The defiant correspondence which now ensued between the governor and the war department doubtless reflected the personal hotheadedness of Troup himself, but Georgia supported her governor and made his

defiances effective. He plainly threatened civil war in case the United States used force to prevent the survey.

On investigation, President Adams reached the conclusion that the treaty was wrongfully secured, and gave orders for a new negotiation. This resulted in the treaty of Washington, in January, 1826, supplemented by that of March, 1826, by which the Creek Indians ceded all of their lands within the state except a narrow strip along the western border. This treaty abrogated the treaty of Indian Springs and it provided that the Indians should remain in possession of their lands until January 1, 1827. Throughout the whole of these proceedings Georgia was bitterly incensed. Claiming that the treaty of Indian Springs became operative after its ratification, and that the lands acquired by it were thereby incorporated with Georgia and were under her sovereignty, the state denied the right of the general government to reopen the question. "Georgia," said Troup, "is sovereign on her own soil," and he entered actively upon the survey of the tract without waiting for the date stipulated in the new treaty. When the surveyors entered the area not ceded by the later treaty, the Indians threatened to use force against them, and at the beginning of 1827 another heated controversy arose. The president warned the governor of Georgia that he should employ, if necessary, "all the means under his control to maintain the faith of the nation by carrying the treaty into effect." Having done this, he submitted the whole matter in a special message to Congress.

"From the first decisive act of hostility," wrote Troup to the secretary of war, "you will be considered and treated as a public enemy"; and he announced his intention to resist any military attack on the part of the United States, "the unblushing allies of the savages." He thereupon made preparations for liberating any surveyors who might be arrested by the United States, and for calling out the militia. In the House of Representatives, a committee recommended the purchase of the Indian title to all lands in Georgia, and, until such cession were procured, the maintenance of the treaty of Washington by all necessary and constitutional means; but the report of the Senate committee, submitted by Benton, supported the idea that the ratification of the treaty of Indian Springs vested the title to the lands in Georgia, and reached the conclusion that no preparations should be made to coerce the state by military force. In November, 1827, the Creeks consented to a treaty extinguishing the last of their claims, and the issue was avoided. . . .

On coming to the Presidency, Jackson was confronted by . . . [this] contest that had arisen between the administration of John Quincy Adams and Georgia over the Indians within the borders of that state. With the attitude characteristic of a Western man and an Indian fighter, Jackson was in hearty sympathy with Georgia, although, in defiance of John Quincy Adams's administration, she had announced advanced ideas on the subject of "state sovereignty." This phrase, however, was used at the time without accurate consideration of its implications, and, when the Cherokees adopted a national constitution, on July 26, 1827, asserting that they were a sovereign and independent nation, with complete jurisdiction over their territory, Georgia countered by an act (December 20, 1828) extending her laws over the entire state, to be fully effective after June 1, 1830. The rush

of gold miners into the Cherokee region raised the question to a critical position, and Jackson withdrew the federal troops, which had been ordered there by the previous administration.

When the subject came before the Supreme Court of the United States, Georgia announced her determination not to appear, nor to allow the Cherokees to exercise authority, but to defend her own sovereignty. The court declined to take jurisdiction, and denied the desired injunction against Georgia. Not until 1832 was the opinion of the court finally expressed, in the case of Worcester v. Georgia. In the decision of the case, Chief Justice John Marshall reached the conclusion that the Cherokees were under the protection of the United States, which had the sole right of managing their affairs, but that they should be recognized as a distinct national state, within the territory of which Georgia's laws could have no force.

On January 3, 1832, however, the House of Representatives of the United States had tabled a resolution to facilitate the enforcement of the decisions of the Supreme Court by federal action. In the Congressional representation of South Carolina, Georgia, Alabama, Mississippi, and Tennessee, only one vote was cast for enforcement of the decisions. Even Kentucky gave as many votes in favor of tabling as against. On the other hand, in Vermont and all of southern New England there was but a single vote (from Connecticut) for tabling. The Middle Atlantic section was divided, the majority, in New York, favoring tabling, but overwhelmingly opposing the motion in Pennsylvania, where the Quaker and missionary friends of the Indians were influential. In all, ninety-nine votes were cast for tabling and eighty-nine against. Jackson's alleged refusal, therefore, to use the power of the federal government against Georgia to enforce the decision of the court was not unwarranted by this action of the House of Representatives. Nevertheless, it was undoubtedly a satisfaction to him to withhold the use of federal troops to carry out "John Marshall's decision." He finally avoided the difficulty by procuring the cession of the disputed lands and the removal of the Indians to the west of the Mississippi.

E. Merton Coulter:

GEORGIA'S DESTINY

E. Merton Coulter is generally considered the most important Georgia historian since Ulrich Bonnell Phillips. It is, therefore, fitting that he should have the last word, not in the controversy over the problems of race relations in a democratic society, but in this sampling of the documents relevant to one small aspect of this seemingly endless and insoluble controversy.

THE Cherokees, living in the mountainous part of the state to the northward, had not got in the way of the Georgians as quickly as had the Creeks; but Georgia was no less conscious of their presence and no less determined that they also must go. In response to the policy, advocated by Jefferson as early as 1803, that the Indians should ultimately be removed to the regions west of the Mississippi, a group of Cherokees had left in 1809 to spy out this new land, and soon returned with a favorable report which led a few to migrate. In 1817 and 1819 they made treaties giving up small strips in northeastern Georgia, and a large number departed, but these were mostly from Tennessee where they had made larger cessions. It seemed that the Georgia Cherokees were less desirous to go than those living in North Carolina, Tennessee, and Alabama.

In 1824, seeing how the Creeks were being pushed out, the Cherokees adopted a definite policy against leaving, and in a memorial to Congress presented by John Ross, George Lowery, Major Ridge, and Elijah Hicks, declared that they knew what the western lands were like—a barren waste with neither trees nor water. There they could engage only in the chase and warfare, and as they had decided to quit those occupations forever, it had now become "the fixed and unalterable determination of this nation never again to cede one foot more of our land." As in the case of the Creeks, there developed a party among the Cherokees, who saw the futility of attempting to hold out against Georgia, and who, therefore, argued that the Cherokees should remove as soon as convenient. This lack of harmony among the Cherokees complicated the problem and led to a long and painful struggle before they were finally forced out.

The United States government, by unwise acts, made more difficult the fulfillment of its promise to Georgia. With one hand it tried to remove the In-

E. Merton Coulter, *Georgia, a Short History* (Chapel Hill: University of North Carolina Press, 1947), pp. 230–237. Reprinted by permission of the publisher.

dians and with the other it planted them deeper into the Georgia soil. In the treaties of 1817 and 1819, it allowed all Cherokees who wanted to become citizens of the United States and who were considered capable of managing their property to receive 640 acres of land and remain in Georgia. It had also, in its efforts to civilize them, aided them with the implements of a stable society, and had helped the American Board of Commissioners for Foreign Missions to Christianize and educate them. To pamper them in the importance that they were taking on as a nation apart from Georgia and in no wise under her control, the United States received Cherokee delegations with all the pomp given to diplomats of foreign nations.

Under such benign influences the Cherokees began to take on a national consciousness and to consider themselves forever implanted in the lower ramparts of their beloved Southern highlands, in a region which had been claimed by Georgians from the day George II had granted it in 1732 but which had belonged to the Indians from time out of mind. They numbered about 14,000. Most of them lived in Georgia, and they owned in 1825 1,277 slaves. Sequoyah, a remarkable Cherokee, invented in 1825 an alphabet; the next year a printing press was set up at New Echota, their capital, which began printing a newspaper, the *Cherokee Phoenix*. The following year they took a long step toward political stability by constructing themselves a constitution and modelling it slightly after the Federal document. A representative of the United States made a trip through the Cherokee country in 1829, and declared that, "the advancement the Cherokees had made in morality, religion, general information and agriculture had astonished him beyond measure. They had regular preachers in their churches, the use of spirituous liquors was in a great degree prohibited, their farms were worked much after the manner of the white people and were generally in good order."

This threat of being deprived of a great part of her domain by an alien and semi-barbarous people appeared intolerable and unthinkable to Georgia; she would resist it to the uttermost limits. Apparently no further dependence could be put in the promise of the United States to remove the Indians, for, going on the assumption that it was not bound to use force, it had not been able to make the Indians cede additional territory for almost a decade. So Georgia started out on a policy which ignored the United States and its futile treaties and which came near ignoring the existence of the Cherokees. John Forsyth, former minister to Spain and now governor, put a swift end to this new nation trying to erect itself in the state of Georgia. He recommended to the legislature that it extend the laws of the state over the Cherokee country, since it was as much a part of Georgia as was the remainder of the state, and that body proceeded to do so on December 20, 1828. Two years later it forbade the Indians to play longer with their make-believe government. Now, there was no longer a Cherokee nation nor were there treaty rights; if the Indians wanted to remain in Georgia they must do so in competition with the whites. Georgia hoped that this new policy of hers would drive them west of the Mississippi.

Georgia, having assumed the government of the Cherokee country, soon found work to do. An Indian named

George Tassel or Corn Tassel was tried for murder in Hall County in 1830 and sentenced to be hanged. Interested friends of the Cherokees had his case carried to the United States Supreme Court on a writ of error; but Georgia, resolving not to be bothered with Federal courts, ordered the sheriff to hang Tassel. George R. Gilmer, who was now governor, declared that he would resist all interference with the Georgia courts.

The Cherokees could get no consolation or sympathy from the imperious Andrew Jackson, president of the United States, for he had been long advising them to accept the inevitable and leave. Even with Georgia ignoring the Cherokee treaty rights, Jackson would not act. With the support of outside friends, the Cherokees sought to have Georgia restrained by the United States Supreme Court, which was dominated by the strong nationalist, John Marshall. In 1830 they sought in that court, through their counsel, William Wirt and John Sergeant, to prevent Georgia from carrying out her laws in the Cherokee country. In this case, known as the Cherokee Nation vs. Georgia, John Marshall held that the Cherokees had no right to bring this suit, not because he did not sympathize with them, but because they were neither citizens nor a foreign nation. Identifying the Indians legally for the first time in American history, he declared that they were a nation subject to the authority of the United States and were its wards. It was clear that the court supported the position of the Indians in their quarrel with Georgia, but it was unable to act in this case, as the suit was not properly before the court. But soon a time would come when it could act.

In July, 1829, gold was discovered in northeastern Georgia, and a stampede set in which filled the diggings with a wild and lawless population. To control them, Federal troops were marched in, and were marched out again when Georgia indicated to her friend, President Jackson, that she did not want them, and that she would manage the region. In 1830 she required all white people in the Cherokee country to secure before March 1st of the following year, a permit to reside there. Though designed primarily to bring to order the lawless gold-diggers, this law also touched the missionaries, who had been working among the Cherokees from the beginning of the century. Even if their own sympathies had not inclined them to the Cherokee position, they would have found it politic in their work with the Indians to agree with them. As a result, the missionaries had become a pernicious influence in the three-cornered imbroglio among Georgia, the Cherokees, and the United States. They had steeled the hearts of the Indians against removal and had brought down upon themselves the hatred of Georgia.

Headstrong and unwise, some of them showed their contempt for Georgia by refusing to call for permits, and invited arrest. The most prominent among them was Samuel A. Worcester. They were tried before Judge Augustin S. Clayton in the Gwinnett County superior court, and released on a technicality, though Judge Clayton was fully determined to resist the Federal government on the main issue. Governor Gilmer, seeking diligently to avoid trouble, begged the missionaries either to accept a permit or to leave the state within ten days. Fanatically indignant that they should be asked to obey the laws of Georgia, they ignored Gilmer's pleas, and as a result, got themselves re-arrested by the Georgia militia and rather roughly handled before they were brought before the Gwinnett court again. Eleven people were arrested, three being missionaries, Samuel A. Worcester, Elizur Butler, and James Trott. They were tried in September, 1831, convicted, and sentenced to four years in the penitentiary. Still desirous of being lenient with them, Governor Gilmer offered each a pardon if he would swear allegiance to Georgia and leave the Cherokee country. All agreed with the exception of Worcester and Butler, who decided they would try to become martyrs.

Besides becoming martyrs, they also hoped to get their case and that of the Cherokee nation before the United States Supreme Court, which they believed would order Georgia out of the Indian country. Worcester, not being an Indian, had the right to bring a case before the court. He entered suit for his freedom in 1831, on the ground that he had violated no law, as Georgia's enactments dealing with the Cherokees were void. The case, known as Worcester *vs.* Georgia, was heard the next year, with Wirt and Sergeant appearing for Worcester. John Marshall now decided that the Georgia acts were void, that she should stop bedevilling the Cherokees, and that she should free Worcester. Wilson Lumpkin, who was now governor and who had important ideas about the Cherokees, paid no attention to Marshall except to say that Georgia would not notice his decision; and President Jackson, who had no love for Marshall, the Indians, or the missionaries, refused to enforce the decision. The missionaries now learning for the first time the astounding fact that Georgia was more powerful than the United States Supreme Court, thought better of their earlier refusal of a pardon, and in January, 1833, accepted the

clemency offered by Governor Lumpkin.

Before the Cherokee troubles were finally settled, Georgia had one more tilt with the Supreme Court, over James Graves, in a case similar to Tassel's. Again she flouted the authority of the Supreme Court and ordered the execution of Graves.

In the meantime, Georgia by other acts was bringing the Cherokee problem to a swift conclusion. In 1831 she ordered the Cherokee lands to be surveyed, the next year she laid them out into ten new counties, and the following year she granted them all away in a lottery. In 1834 she allowed the whites to go in and occupy their holdings, and gave the Cherokees two years to get out of the way. Not only were the Cherokees maneuvered out of Georgia, but the United States was forced into a corner where it was necessary for her to act. Most of the Cherokees were wise enough to see that they should make a treaty and leave as soon as possible. Their representatives went to Washington in 1834 and made a treaty, but a faction, headed by John Ross, a Scotch half-breed, refused to accept it, as they were determined never to leave Georgia. The next year another treaty was made, but the Cherokees refused to accept it in a council they held at Running Water. In December of that year, United States commissioners came to New Echota, the Cherokee capital, and made a treaty with the faction led by John Ridge, Major Ridge, and Elias Boudinot, who saw the futility of holding out longer. The Ross followers refused to appear and opposed the treaty. By this treaty the Cherokees agreed to give up all their lands and in return to migrate to lands in the West and receive $5,000,000.

In 1838 the Cherokees, rounded up by

the hard methods of the United States troops under General Scott, set out for their western home, giving up forever the Georgia hills, which they had so well loved and for which they had fought so long. A small group were able to elude the law and the army and finally to gain a legal footing in a reservation in western North Carolina, where they have ever afterwards kept alive their ancient manners and customs.

Georgia's long struggle with the Indians was of widespread interest, not only to her own citizens but also to the people of the United States. It upset Congress frequently and brought into play the oratory of Clay, Webster, and Calhoun as well as the heated clashes of others. It became a subject of angry conversation among abolitionist groups and Northern sewing circles, and led to the widening of the ugly rift of sectionalism, which slavery had already created. Georgia heard enough to make her resent Northerners coming south to exploit these troubles. Mistaking John Howard Payne's visit to the Cherokees as outside meddling, she invaded Tennessee to arrest him, and held him prisoner until his mission was better understood.

Though Georgia was not the only state to have Indians, she had greater difficulty than any other in getting rid of them or settling the question of their status, despite the fact that the United States was under special obligations to her to remove them. Through treaties negotiated by 1832, Mississippi had been given the promise of freedom from her Choctaws and Chickasaws; Florida, from her Seminoles; and Alabama, from her Creeks. Georgia still had her Cherokees, with a few in North Carolina, Tennessee, and Alabama, and it seemed to her that she was destined to have them forever. She acted vigorously throughout the whole contest, and early took the lead in a struggle which she carried on with such success that it was unnecessary for the neighboring states to raise the issue.

It had happened that more through natural developments than design, the United States had cleared out most of the Indians from the states north of the Mason and Dixon Line and of the Ohio River, while they still remained in great strength in the South. This led Georgia to charge sectional partiality.

With the Indians finally out of the way, Georgia was for the first time in her existence master of her own territorial destiny. Now she was unshackled; with exuberance and enthusiasm she could now go forward.

Suggestions for Additional Reading

The "Jacksonian Era" is almost entirely different from the "Era of Reform," though they bear the same dates. The former was expeditious, for the most part, and respectful of the attitudes of its slaveholding, Irish, and other supporters. The latter was moral and humanitarian, as in its temperance and abolitionist concerns. Both are seen best in the common frame of the multivolumed histories of the period, especially John Bach MacMaster's *History of the People of the United States*, especially Volumes Six and Seven (New York, 1906, 1910), which treat numerous movements and events, including the Cherokee controversy, with vivid detail.

There is a large bibliography of writings on both Andrew Jackson and John Marshall. John Spencer Bassett's two-volume *Life of Andrew Jackson* (Garden City, 1911) and Marquis James' *Andrew Jackson: Portrait of a President* (Indianapolis, 1937) remain the most useful; William MacDonald, *Jacksonian Democracy, 1828–1837* (New York, 1906) strives to be fair to Jackson, but concedes the illogical nature of his Indian policy. Albert J. Beveridge's four-volume *Life of John Marshall* (Boston, 1919) is one of the most famous of all American biographies. James A. Servies, ed., *A Bibliography of John Marshall* (Washington, 1956), was prepared for his Bicentennial, and is indexed for ready use. Edward S. Corwin's *John Marshall and the Constitution* (New Haven, 1919) is short, but both readable and authoritative. Richard Longaker, "Andrew Jackson and the Judiciary," *Political Science Quarterly*, LXXXI (1956), 341–364, emphasizes that Jackson opposed Marshall, not, as popularly supposed, the Supreme Court.

Of the numerous histories of the State of Georgia, E. Merton Coulter's *Georgia, a Short History* (Chapel Hill, 1933) is most readily available. Ulrich Bonnell Phillips' *Georgia and State Rights* (Washington, 1902) is a balanced and scholarly study of Georgia from the Revolution to the Civil War. The emphasis is on Georgia's relations with the Federal Government. Students seeking a more detailed study of the intricacies of state politics should consult Paul Murray, *The Whig Party in Georgia, 1825–1853* (Chapel Hill, 1948). Milton Sydney Heath's *Constructive Liberalism* (Cambridge, Mass., 1954) is rich in data pertaining to many aspects of economic life in Georgia from 1732 to 1860. Wilson Lumpkin's autobiography, *The Removal of the Cherokees* (2 vols., New York, 1907), is fascinating and filled with useful documents, but is not readily obtainable. Robert McPherson's brief biography of Lumpkin (and a defense of his policies) appears in Horace Montgomery's collection, *Georgians in Profile* (Athens, Georgia, 1958), pp. 144–167. Studies of George R. Gilmer and of George M. Troup are quite unreliable: the standard works are Gilmer, *Sketches of Some of the First Settlers of Upper Georgia, of the Cherokees, and the Au-*

thor (New York, 1855), and Edward J. Harden, *The Life of George McIntosh Troup* (Savannah, 1859). One of the best descriptions of daily life in Georgia is found in Augustus Baldwin Longstreet's *Georgia Scenes* (1835), a lively, irreverent, and amusing series of short fictional sketches originally published in local newspapers, and available in numerous editions.

The literature on the Cherokee is large. Notable for the period just preceding the clash between Indians and states-rights partisans is R. S. Cotterill, *The Southern Indians: The Story of the Civilized Tribes Before Removal* (Norman, 1954). Marion L. Starkey's *The Cherokee Nation* (New York, 1946) is a well-written narrative based on wide research. Miss Starkey tells the story of the Cherokee from the earliest times through the crisis of the removal. Thomas V. Parker's *The Cherokee Indians* (New York, 1907), a concise account, is carefully derived from Government documents. Among the Cherokee chiefs, Sequoyah was unique: a humanist of whom any people might be proud, a living argument against removal. He is treated in George E. Foster, *Se-Quo-Yah: the American Cadmus and Modern Moses* (Philadelphia, 1885); Grant Foreman, *Sequoyah* (Norman, Okla., 1938); and Henry T. Malone, *Cherokees of the Old South* (Athens, Ga., 1956), pp. 153–170, as well as in other works already mentioned. Three books published by the University of Oklahoma Press (Norman, Okla.) provide additional insights and interesting reading: Althea Bass's *The Cherokee Messenger* (1936), a study of the Rev. Samuel A. Worcester; Ralph Henry Gabriel's *Elias Boudinot, Cherokee, and His America* (1941), a moving biography of a tragic figure; Ed-

ward E. Dale and Gaston Litton's *Cherokee Cavaliers: Forty Years of Cherokee History as Told in the Correspondence of the Ridge-Watie-Boudinot Family* (1939), an excellent documentary history. The earliest trustworthy study of the drama of Indian removal is Anne Heloise Abel's *The History of Events Resulting in Indian Consolidation West of the Mississippi* (Washington, 1908). The best study of Indian removal, by an outstanding ethnologist and historian in the field, is Grant Foreman's illustrated volume, *Indian Removal: the Emigration of the Five Civilized Tribes of Indians* (Norman, Okla., 1932; new ed., 1953). The Cherokee removal is treated on pp. 229–312.

Students who wish to deal with original sources will find *Gales and Seaton's Register of Debates in Congress* and J. D. Richardson's *Compilation of the Messages and Papers of the Presidents* available in most college libraries. Both of these sources are indexed. The scholarly student will then consult the various volumes of *American State Papers*. The complete text of the Georgia Cession of April 24, 1802, is, for instance, published in the class *Public Lands*, I, 125–126. The class *Indian Affairs* provides a documentary history until 1827. The texts of the various treaties with the Cherokee (and other tribes) are available in Charles J. Kappler's *Indian Affairs: Laws and Treaties* (2 vols., Washington, 1903), published as *Senate Document No. 452, 57th Congress, 1st Session*. The student concerned to know the daily life of the educated citizen of Jacksonian America will find much of interest, on every conceivable topic, by following the Cherokee controversy through the pages of *Niles' Weekly Register*, a leading journal of the day.

The Cherokee controversy provided only one of numerous problems in the relationship between Indians and white men, some of which continue to require attention. The Office of Indian Affairs, Department of the Interior, publishes varied materials on phases of its operations. A valuable compilation of articles on controversial questions involving Indians is Walter M. Daniels, comp., *American Indians* (New York, 1957).